# The Zen
## of Modern Life
## and the
## Reality of Reality

Scott Shaw

Buddha Rose Publications

The Zen of Modern Life
and the Reality of Reality
Copyright © 2013 by Scott Shaw
www.scottshaw.com
ALL RIGHTS RESERVED

This book contains material protected under International and Federal Copyright Laws and Treaties. Any unauthorized reprint or use of this material is prohibited. No part of this book may be reproduced or transmitted in any form or by any means, electronic or mechanical, including photocopying, recording, or by any information storage and retrieval system without express written permission from the author or publisher.

Front Cover Calligraphy by Scott Shaw
Copyright © 2013 All Rights Reserved

Rear Cover Photograph of Scott Shaw
by Hae Won Shin
Copyright ©2013 All Rights Reserved

First Edition 2013
Second Edition 2025

ISBN: 1-877792-69-1
ISBN 13: 9781877792694

Library of Congress Control Number:
2013943474

Printed in the United States of America

10 9 8 7 6 5 4 3 2 1

*The Zen of Modern Life
and the Reality of Reality*

*Contents*

| | |
|---|---|
| Introduction | 9 |
| The Reality of Reality | 11 |
| What is enlightenment? | 12 |
| Reality and the Spiritual Path | 17 |
| The Signs and The Mirrors | 20 |
| Does It Make Them Better? | 22 |
| The Sanga | 24 |
| Anger | 30 |
| Evolutionary Choice | 33 |
| Patterns | 38 |
| What Are You Thinking? | 41 |
| Large or Small | 43 |
| The Near-Death Experience | 45 |
| Pranayama | 49 |
| In Your Own Moment | 51 |
| Things You Will Never Know | 56 |
| Interpretation | 62 |
| Roller-Girl | 69 |
| There is No, "Me," in Service | 71 |
| Consciousness Verse Oblivion: Choice Verse Ego | 75 |
| The Master | 77 |
| Life Happens in a Second | 80 |
| Sins of the Father | 82 |
| Things You Will Never Know | 86 |
| How People Craft Their Life | 92 |
| Life is Defined by Availability | 97 |

| | |
|---|---|
| Why Do You Believe? | 102 |
| I'm Glad You Received Your Karma For What You Did But How Does That Help Me? | 105 |
| You Hold All of These Things in Your Mind | 107 |
| Your Own Agenda | 110 |
| Meditation is Everywhere | 114 |
| Higher Consciousness: A Study in Fiction | 117 |
| God's Job | 122 |
| The Birth of Karma | 126 |
| What Happens When It Doesn't Work? | 129 |
| Control IT or IT Controls You | 131 |
| Buying Into Their Own B.S. | 135 |
| Sometimes You Have to Adapt | 140 |
| Why Don't You Take the Time to Actually Achieve Something In Your Life? | 142 |
| Positive or Negative | 146 |
| Karma Heavy People | 150 |
| The Meditative Pathway to Insanity | 154 |
| Why a Guru is Bad | 157 |
| What Are You Basing Your Knowledge Upon? | 161 |
| What If You Didn't Know? | 163 |
| Just Because You Pass the Information Onto Somebody Doesn't Mean That They Understand It | 166 |
| You Get What You Pay For | 167 |

| | |
|---|---|
| How You Measure Time? | 169 |
| Hello! This is Reality | 171 |
| You'll See When You See. You'll Know When You Know. | 173 |
| The Earth Still Spins | 175 |
| Books by Scott Shaw | 179 |

*Introduction*

Zen emerged onto the world as a Buddhist concept. Born in Buddhism, it rose initially from Hinduism—as *Siddhartha Gautama, The Sakyamuni Buddha,* was a Hindu. From his enlightenment he taught his understanding(s) to his followers. From this, a new religion was founded.

As time traveled forward and the understanding of what *The Buddha* spoke moved across the globe, the initial Buddhist teachings came to be influenced by other philosophical understandings. From China, *Taoism* was intermingled and came to form an essential basis for the birth of Zen which initially flourished in Japan.

Zen has continued to move forward throughout the centuries and be expounded across the globe.

With each new generation that is exposed to Zen new understandings and techniques are embraced.

These understandings and techniques are designed to guide the aspirants towards the ultimate level of human consciousness, enlightenment.

At its heart, Zen is a method of removing the veils of illusion from an individual's life in order that they may gain a clearer perspective of Life, the Universe, and the Self. Within the pages of this book, Scott Shaw presents just that, thought-provoking and thought-silencing ideas which are designed to guide the reader towards a clearer understanding of Self in order that they may gain a glimpse of the supreme knowledge, *Nirvana*.

## The Reality of Reality

For those who walk the *Path of the World* they expect, and in some cases anticipate, *Badness*. Bad has been done to them. They have done bad to others. It is a dog-eat-dog world so you have to do whatever you can to get over.

For those on the *Spiritual Path* they do not expect, anticipate, or in many cases even understand *Badness*. When it occurs, they question, *"Why,"* and are, in fact, oftentimes dumbfounded by it. They seek good. They do good. So, why should anything but good happen to them?

And, this is a GOOD question.

The reality is, if you do good things, say good things, act goodly, good things will, (for the most part), follow you. Just as if you do negative things, say negative things, act badly, (no matter what your justification), *Badness* will seek you out.

You can run, but you can't hide.

People occasionally question me, *"Why when I speak or when I write do I detail some of the more mundane aspects of life?"* The answer is, This is LIFE! We are all defined by the same set of elements. And, you can chalk Life-Events up to karma, destiny, or god testing you all you want... But, here we are. This is it. We each create our own reality based upon how we encounter life and how we treat other people in this life. We will each reap what we have sewn. But, beyond that, life is going to happen. The bad will occasionally receive good and the good will occasionally receive bad. This is the reality of reality. As such, this is what I discuss.

## What is Enlightenment?

*What is enlightenment?*

Stop reading right now and take a few moments to define, in your own mind, how you describe enlightenment.

**Enlightenment**

For those of us who walk the *Spiritual Path,* the ideology of enlightenment is central to our path of spiritual unfolding. Whether it is the ultimate sought after goal or something you think you will never achieve, it is a concept that is deeply embedded in our minds. In fact, how you define enlightenment is one of the primary elements that will come to guide you on your path of evolution. It is for this reason that you must clearly define, in your own mind, what you THINK enlightenment is.

There is no right or wrong answer to, *"What is enlightenment?"* Throughout time and the various religious traditions the concept has been defined in different ways. For those of us on the *Spiritual Path* we have no doubt heard differing definitions and ideas taught about enlightenment.

The reality is, however, no matter what someone else claims enlightenment to be, it is only YOU who can take these various definitions and come to your own ultimate conclusion—defining for yourself what you consider enlightenment to BE.

At the end of the day, just as your life is defined by you, so too is such a vast concept as enlightenment. Take some time and decide what you consider enlightenment to be.

**The Consensus**

For many, enlightenment is some far-off mindset that can only be embraced by the most pure and the most holy. This is what is taught in many religious traditions.

The problem with this definition of enlightenment is, however, that it keeps people separate from its obtainment. And, this is not good.

In Zen, it is understood that we each are ALREADY enlightened; we simply need to remember and re-embrace this fact. Many people, however, through cultural and religious programming feel unworthy to embrace this understanding.

Instead, many leave enlightenment to some other person or to some other time in their life when they have reached that place of, *"Older and wiser."* The reality is, if you do not accept your perfection in every moment of your life, that, *"Older and wiser,"* will never appear. You will simply pass through life and then your life will be gone.

All THINGS are HERE in this moment. This is especially the case with spiritual knowledge. You simply need to open your mind up to this fact and then the understanding which is at the root of Zen, *"That we all ARE already enlightened,"* may be embraced.

**The Other Side of the Issue**
On the other side of the issue is that many people define enlightenment as some state of overall perfection where there is none of the human interactions that we each face on a daily basis in our lives. Many people believe that the enlightened individual is in such a perfect state of grace that all things simply come to them: be in money, housing, food, guidance from god, and all of the etcetera. And, to a certain degree that is true. For in the state of embraced enlightenment all things are witnessed as perfect; as such, life does take on a perfect state of grace.

But, this understanding can be deceiving—especially when it is used as a means to define enlightenment.

From the dawn of advancing human consciousness forward, the stories have been told about the perfect enlightened individual who is in such perfect communion with the absolute that all they do is sit and meditate all day, every day. If they have any needs they are seen to by their disciples. Perhaps, to a certain degree, for an enlightened master who lives in a monastery, this may be the visual image that is projected. But, at the root of humanity is that we ALL have similar needs, and to sustain human life these needs must be met.

That is reality. It does not take away from a person's enlightenment.

This also brings us to another point in the definition of enlightenment. Many of those people who were described as being perfectly enlightened died long ago. When a person is no longer in their body all kinds of things can be written and said about them. But, these are just words. If you do not personally interact with an individual you can never personally know who that person was or was not. Therefore, it is essential to let go of idol worship if you wish to truly embrace your own enlightenment.

**In Your Own Time**

Enlightenment is lived in your own time. It is defined by you with the knowledge you possess. If you wish to understand/embrace enlightenment you must let go of definitions that keep you from achieving it.

*Let go and know.*
*Embrace it and know it.*

As long as you separate yourself from enlightenment by feeling that you are not worthy or that you are not ready, it will always be distant from you.

As long as you separate yourself from enlightenment by surrounding yourself with people who tell you that you are not enlightened and you must perform this technique or that technique for years upon years or even through multiple incarnations before it may be achieved, it will always be distant from you.

As long as you separate yourself from enlightenment by believing that an enlightened person does not have to deal with the mundane necessity of life, it will always be distant from you.

Enlightenment can be felt by you RIGHT NOW. Enlightenment can be felt by you everyday. Yes, even when you are doing your laundry, walking the dog, washing your dishes, or dealing with someone who just cut you off and yelled at you as you are driving down the street.

Enlightenment is alive every day. Let go of definitions that hold you back from experiencing it and embrace the light.

## Reality and the Spiritual Path

Just as with the concept of enlightenment, many people believe that by walking the *Spiritual Path* they will somehow be removed from the trials and the tribulations of life. Certainly, with a spiritual mindset most will possess a better set of tools to deal with reality than the average person who fights their way through a life dominate only by desire and the fulfillment of those momentary cravings.

This being stated, you will encounter obstacles even if your feet are firmly planted on the *Spiritual Path*. This is the reality of life.

Some people when they encounter some form of life-reality that they are not particularly happy with they choose to believe, *"They are being tested."* But, this is just mental nonsense—a justification for the *Reality of Reality*.

*Why would anybody be testing you?*

The simple fact of the matter is, life is life. There are so many people doing so many things—all based in their own desires for what they want or what they hope to achieve that is inevitable that you will encountered someone or something that will cross your path and challenge your peace.

I often detail evens that have taken place in my own life to illustrate this fact. The fact is that we all encounter Life-Things that we do not like. No one is immune.

And, the more you are out there in life, the stronger the chance that these life events will occur. This is why some on the *Spiritual Path* choose to retreat to monasteries and live a life sheltered from the world. For within walls the chances of dealing with the *Reality of Reality* are far diminished.

Personally, I too have spent time in a monastery—locked deeply within the walls of a religious group. One of the first things that shocked me was when I came to realize that there were personality conflicts within those walls, as well.

At the time I came to realize this I was sixteen years old and full of all of the youthful exuberance of someone newly walking the formalized *Spiritual Path*. Though it shocked me at the time, it also caused me to realize that this is the reality of life and particularly the reality of life on the *Spiritual Path*. ...No matter how much you attempt to run and hide to be spiritual, the reality of life, ego, desire, and the definitions of humanity will come to find you. Thus, there will be personality conflicts.

It is important to understand that this is not bad or good. It is simply life. And, in life we are destined to deal with Life-Stuff. So, running and/or hiding is never the answer. Sure, it can be nice to give yourself a break from the daily grind. But, it will never free you from the Human Condition.

This being said, the ultimate truth is, all you can do is live your life as spiritually and as consciously as possible. When Life-Stuff comes at you, do what you can do to keep your focus on your spirituality—keep your gaze on the enlightenment and try to gain new realizations and learn from the experiences you are experiencing. Perhaps you will even learn a method to keep yourself from dealing with that same type of experience ever again.

The reality of life on the *Spiritual Path* is that we each ultimately realize that we are no different—certainly no better than anyone else. All we are is someone who embraces the cosmos and seeks to make sense of the actions that take place in this place we call, *"Life."*

So, when something comes at you that you do not like. And, it will come. Stay conscious, step back from the emotions that surround it, (especially if they are negative emotions), and embrace the essence of who you are—a spiritual being.

## The Signs and The Mirrors

Every negative thing that will happen to you in your life will be prescreened in front of your eyes before it ever occurs. This may happen in a number of forms. Someone may be talking and they will say something that is a warning of what is to come. Though they may have no thought that they are sending you a message, it will none-the-less be revealed to you. Or, you may see an occurrence. In this case, it is a foreshadowing of events that will come to pass in your own life.

This is a very complicated understanding to come to terms with. And, it takes a very astute mind to differentiate between *Magical Thinking,* (head-tripping), and *True Realization.* Meaning, you must train your mind to be aware of the signs when they are presented to you and not allow yourself to simply becoming a paranoid mess.

How do you do this? There is no one method. What you simply have to do is to study the events of your life. Then, look back through your history and see when you were warned before a situation presented itself. In each case, you will remember something you heard or a sight you saw that could have prevented you from taking the actions you did that lead you onto and through the negative Life-Event. From this practice, you will gain the insight to know when you are being warned.

Again, this is a very sublet metaphysical science. I won't go into the whys and the wherefores of the reason(s) this occurs in each of our lives, but to come to work with this understanding you must become very self-aware and interactive with the divine *karmic* interaction(s) of this Life-Place.

**The Mirrors**

More than simply signs of what is to come there are also, *The Mirrors*. These allow YOU to witness YOU through the actions of others. Meaning, you will be allowed to see yourself: The Self that was and The Self that is to come, in the actions of other people.

To understand the practice of mirrors, you will need to take the time to study Life-Actions. Namely, the behavior of those other people you encounter—even if you only see them from across a street.

If you watch humanity, you will witness the WAY people behave. This can guide you in two ways. One, it will allow you to see how not to react when certain life situations present themselves to you. And two, your actions will be mimicked, repeated by others. From this, you can see how badly or how goodly you behaved at certain points in your life and learn what actions to take or not to take when encountering the same type of situation in the future.

A deeper understanding of life is always available for those who take the time to study True Reality.

## Does It Make Them Better?

There always have and there always will be people out there who will state, *"I don't do that!"* Be it, they don't cuss, drink alcohol, smoke, eat meat, drink caffeine, have sex, whatever...

When they make this statement, and particularly when they decide not to do what they do not do, they base their ideology upon that fact that not doing makes them *Something More, Something Better.* Even if it is a very subtle decision not to do something, it is based upon the ideology that by not doing they are better than someone who does.

Now this, *"Better,"* may be based upon physically, psychologically, morally, spiritually, psychically, or any number of other *...ally's.* But, does, *"Not doing,"* truly make a person better?

From a spiritual perspective there has been a very long tradition of telling people what not to do. *"Not doing,"* supposedly make the person closer to god or more in-tune with the ways of the universe. But, all understandings taught by man, (or woman), are based upon what is known and/or believed at a specific period of time. And, what is known at a particular period of time is based upon the morality and culture of a particular place, in a specific placement in time and geography. This morality then influences the research and the acceptance of the prevailing scientific knowledge of a particular time in history.

Ultimately, time changes the understandings of science. Time changes the practices of culture. Time changes everything—particularly what we consider to be factual knowledge.

Thus, with everything in a constant state of change, there is no absolute of what is or is not RIGHT.

To the person who, *"Does not."* What they do or do not is what they do. What they do or do not is done for themselves.

Does doing what they don't do give them self-discipline? Probably. Does what they don't do make them more healthy? Maybe. Does their not doing what they don't do make the world a better place? Possibly.

But, at the end of the day, what they don't do is what they don't do. It is not you and it is not me. What they do not do does not make them better or more than you or I. It simply makes them who they are.

## The Sanga

In the Buddhist tradition it is taught that the *Sanga* or *Spiritual Community* is one of the primary elements that one should take into consideration as they walk upon the *Spiritual Path*. To put this understanding into plainer language, the *Sanga* refers to the fact that, *"You can know a person by the company that they keep."* Worldly people associate with worldly people and spiritual people associate with spiritual people.

Throughout all spiritual traditions a person is told that they should let go of worldly friends and only associate with spiritual, like-minded people. On the surface, this sounds like a pretty good idea.

Think about it... For the most part a spiritually inclined person is probably not going to get you into too much trouble as they probably don't drink, do drugs, womanize or manize, don't party, and don't do worldly activities that may have the tendency to lead you down the road to demise. Thus, you will probably remain fairly safe.

But, at this juncture, as we study the concept of *Sanga,* the questions have to be raised, *"What exactly is spiritual?"* And, *"Who is truly a spiritual person?"*

This is the point where the novice on the *Spiritual Path* oftentimes becomes confused. For what appears to be spiritual is not always the truest representation of spirituality. And, those who appear to be holy are not necessarily that.

Here in the West, the obvious examples of this are the priests who mess with young children. On all levels that is just wrong! There is no excuse and no justification for that type of action!

Though these inappropriate actions have been at the forefront of the news over the past couple of decades, these actions have literally gone on forever. And, they have spanned all cultures and all religious traditions.

In fact, it is so common that a person in a position of religious authority takes advantage of a person that it has seemingly become commonly accepted knowledge. That is simply sad. Add to this that these people are supposedly representatives of god or whatever figure a particular religion places as its most holy. From this, these people are provided with a license to do pretty much whatever they want and claim it as an act of god.

Here lies one of the primary problems with the concept of *Sanga*.
At its heart, the *Sanga* ideology is fine. But, then add to it the desirous-mind of the human personality and then any spiritual concept it may provide is completely lost.

Watch the news when a priest or other religious figure is accused of inappropriate behavior and you will always see people stepping up in the defense of that person. *"I don't believe it!" They are too nice—too holy to do anything like that!"* Then, when the accusations are proven to be true, the statements change, *"I can't believe it. He seemed like such a good man."* And so on...

On the other side of the issue, as this type of behavior has become so prevalent, there are people who falsely claim that a person did something inappropriate to them. When, in fact, they did not. An individual does this simply to either take control over a person's life or to make them seem less pure or spiritual to the masses. This may be based in anger, jealously, or an untold number of other emotions. But, at the end of the day it creates the same Life-Problem attributed to that of the wayward priest; namely, the actions of another destroy and forever alter the life of another person.

This type of action is similar to the situations that took place back in the 1970s when the penalties for drug possession were much more severe. If someone happened to be upset with another person, an action they may take would be to buy some drugs and then plant them in the person's car or in their apartment. At this point they would call the police and report the person. As technology was much less advanced then, it would be very difficult to find out who the reporting person actually was. Thus, the police would go to the location, find the drugs, and arrest the person upon whom the drugs had been planted. Though the individual actually had done nothing wrong, their life was forever altered—even if they did beat the charge.

Though these examples are not all that common, they do exist. Why is this? Because each person has their own agenda. At one point they may be your friend and your biggest supporter. The next moment they may completely hate you.

Emotions change. People change. When a person's desires are not being met, some go to outlandish ends to seek revenge.

**People**

At the root of the *Sanga* are people. People by their very nature—their very design, are flawed.

The human race is based upon desire. People desire THINGS. These things may be physical, they may be spiritual. But, desire is the root-cause of all things both good and bad in this place we call Life.

Some people desire objects. Some people desire love. Some people desire lust. Some people desire fulfillment. Some people desire enlightenment. But, no matter what the title, *Desire is Desire*.

Though it is commonly understood that a *Sanga* is made up of specified group of spiritual people who desire the same end-goal. But, do they?

Each person comes to the *Sanga* with his or her own unique set of life experiences. Each person comes to the *Sanga* with his or her own personality. Each person comes to the *Sanga* with his or her own set of desires. And, though they may each be seeking a similar end-goal, they each may desire a similar communal experience—each person is a unique and different entity. As such they each add a particular set of variables to the overall equation.

A *Sanga* is measured by the overall output of its amassed energy. Add one faulty person to a *Sanga* and that energy is damaged and altered forever.

Each and every action we take not only affects ourselves and the overall evolution of our life, but it also affects any of those we have interaction with.

What you do today equals the choices you will be presented with tomorrow.

Who you encounter today, leads you to the people you will interact with tomorrow.

As each person is their own unique entity, you can never anticipate, never assume what actions they will make from moment-to-moment. As such, though they may present themselves as a spiritual person, that image can never truly define who or what they are.

The *Sanga,* in its concept, is an idealize image of a perfect community and support group. Though it sounds nice and no doubt can provide a positive learning experience. You must always keep your guard up; as you can never know what actions another person may take.

Ultimately, true spiritually is never defined by how a person appears to the world. True spiritually is only known internally. It is only defined by the True-Inner-Self.

Find it in you. Not outside of you.

## *Anger*

Most spiritual traditions detail that anger is a bad thing—that one should repress it and work to overcome it. Though there is a lot to be said about not being angry—because when does anger make you happy? The other side of the issue is, *repression is never a good thing.* Though you may hide the emotion of anger, repression does not make that emotion go way.

Many people assume that in spiritual communities there is never confrontation based upon anger. This is not the case. As someone who has spent a lot of time in *ashrams* and spiritual centers, I can tell you from personal experience that there is still interpersonal confrontation based upon anger. People, even spiritual ones, still get mad and still argue.

But, what is anger?

Anger is you not getting what you want from a specific person or a situation. The reason you become angry is that your desires are not being met.

You want something. You want a specific desired outcome. But, you are not getting what you want. Thus, you become angry.

Therefore, anger is based in you. It is based in what you desire.

Now, some people are psychologically mature enough to understand this fact and, thus, they look deeply into their self and understand that they may desire an outcome that is not being met but they turn this realization into a *sadhana,* a spiritual practice, and they use it to refine their own consciousness.

Some are very good at doing this. They are very mentally evolved, and their actions are not based in the suppression of anger but instead upon a much higher level of consciousness where they can see beyond the desirousness of their individual-self. Most of us are not like that, however. Periodically, we get pissed off.

Ultimately, getting mad is not the issue. What you do with the energy of anger is what becomes the issue.

How many people have done very-very bad things due to their anger? Many people have spent their life in jail due to anger. Many people have drastically altered the life of another person, in a very negative manner, due to anger. And, so on…

So, you have to decide how you are going to treat anger when it arises in your life. You need to consciously make this choice if you hope to stay free from the negative *karma* of anger. But, how do you do this?

The main thing is, you must stay conscious. Realize you are angry; witness it, but do not become overcome by it. In other words, control your anger as opposed to being control by your anger.

The fact is, every now and then it feels good to yell when you are mad. It is a great cathartic release. In fact, sometimes it takes yelling at a person to actual get them to listen to your point of view. But, sometimes yelling at them will only equal them become mad at you for your being mad at them. This is not good or bad. It is simply the way it is.

The main thing is, if you desire to live a focused, conscious life, you must keep your anger in check. You must realize that when you are angry, you are angry because YOU are not getting what YOU want. To go to this space of self-understanding when you are mad will immediately separate you from the controlling hands of anger. By stepping back and looking into yourself and your reasoning for being angered, frees you. It gives you the perspective you need to not simply become a screaming spoiled child but, instead, a more understanding person in term of not only the other people you are involved with but life itself.

## *Evolutionary Choice*

Throughout the evolution of human consciousness there have been a lot of saying and/or slogans that have been spoken. Some have come to be used over-and-over-and-over again. From this, they have come to be a believed metaphor. Near the top of this list is the saying, *"You only get one shot."* Meaning, you only get one chance to make something of your life, but if you don't, it is all downhill from that point.

Think about it. How many times have you heard that saying or a similar one?

Many people say it. Many people believe. But, is it true?

**Choices**

We all make choices in our lives. Sometimes we choose to go this way. Sometimes we choose to go that way. The reality of choice is, however, once a choice is made, it sets the next set of evolutionary choices and circumstances in motion in your life.

For example, sometimes we make a choice and are so happy with the outcome. In other cases, once we have made a choice, we realize that it was a very bad choice, and we should have followed a different path. But, the choice was made. And, by making it, it has come to define the next set of circumstances in our life.

Life is made up of choices. It is as simple as that. Some choices we make we will be very happy with. Others, we will wish we had not made.

But, this is reality. This is life.

No one is happy with every choice that they make. But, choice is one of the most dominant factors of human existence.

**Choice and Desire**

The choices we make are predominated defined by desire. We want something. We want a desired outcome. We want a desired object. So, we make the choices we believe will allow us to obtain that object.

The problem is, until you have obtained that desired object you never know what owning it will mean. Whether that object is a thing, a person, an occupation, or a level of achievement—until you own it, you can never truly understand what the choices you made to get it will equal.

This is kind of like the American folklore analogy of the singer who travels to the crossroads to sell their soul to the devil to become a famous musician. They sign the contract, they get what they were promised, but the outcome of fame is completely different than they thought.

This is like life. There are all kinds of subtle costs for obtaining any desire you have that can never be anticipated. Thus, many people are left realizing that they got what they thought that they wanted, but now they no longer desire to pay the costs and be defined by their original desire. But, it is too late. They already made their deal with the devil.

In life, we all want things. So, we go about obtaining them. Once we get them, however, we often realize that their ownership is not at all what we had anticipated.

For example, someone meets a person and falls in love. They enter into a relationship with the person but then it all goes bad. It ends, and they are very sorry they ever met or desired the person because of all the negativity that the relationship has cost them. This same scenario goes onto employment goals, possessions, and everything else.

The reality is, you cannot know what a desire will equal until it is lived. And, once you live it, it may destroy you. But, you made the choices to get to that end-goal. So, who is to blame?

**Choice and Reality**

Choice is one of the subtlest components of life. And, all choice are not as all-encompassing as the previously detailed ones. Choices are also driven by life necessity. For example, someone makes a choice to go to the supermarket. They get in their car and on their way to the store get into a car wreck. A choice, yes. But, it was defined by an unanticipated outcome.

This is the other reality of life in association with choice. There are a zillion people, animals, objects, and acts of nature that can never be charted or anticipated. They exist in their own sphere of reality, just as you do. So, while you are doing what you do; so are they. And, the two of you may come into unexpected contact. This is life.

**Circumstances**

As stated, what a choice does is to set the next set of circumstances of your life into motion. Your choices cause your evolution. And, good or bad is what you make of the outcome of each choice. But, good or bad is not wholly defined by you receiving a specific, desired outcome.

As I have long discussed, it is you who decides what to do with the life circumstances you are handed. It is you who decides to become held back and hindered by them or to learn from them and move forward. Like I say, *"If you love Hell, it becomes Heaven."*

This being stated, in life you must make choices. These choices will be fueled by your desires. And, do not get it wrong; even the most spiritual of people have desires. They desire *god-consciousness* or *nirvana*. That too is a desire. So, as material as your desires may be, they are no less holy than that of the monk. They are just desires. Desires are the byproduct of life. And, these desires will set your life in motion by the choices you make to obtain them.

Whatever happens is whatever happens. A choice turning bad or transforming into a believed opportunity missed, does not need to define your entire existence. What defines your life is what you do next. And, *"Next,"* is available until you die.

Here is the reality. You get a lot more than one shot in life!

## *Patterns*

People who are not happy with the course of their life frequently question me wondering how they can consciously turn their existence around. The reason people get locked into a life that they are not happy with is that they enter into a pattern and then they do not attempt to change that pattern.

Each of us enters a Life-Path when we are young. Many of us never take a look at that path until we reach a point in our life where we are truly dissatisfied. But, by then, that pattern may be too deeply embedded in the structure of our life, making it very difficult, if not impossible, to change.

Life is like a river flowing to the sea. When it is new, the path it follows is not deeply embedded. But, as time goes on, that river continues to carve deeper and deeper into the landscape until it has created a very deep canyon. Then, climbing to the top of the sheer walls of that canyon to escape is never easy. It is doable, but it is not easy.

This is why when a person is young they need to take a long hard look at what they are creating with their life and where it will lead them. The problem is, youth is filled with the promises of tomorrow. So, few young people truly take the time to envision what their tomorrow will look like if they continue down the road they are currently on.

I think we have all seen people who walk down the street with their shoulders sloped over and their eyes staring towards the ground; beaten by life. I think we all have met people who are very-very negative and angry at what life has feed them. But, at the source of all this is the choices they made and the road they choose to walk down many years ago.

The source of your life is you. It is the choices you have made.

If you want to change your life, you must change your behavior. If you want your life to different, you must change your patterns.

It is you who has set a course of events in motion in your life. If you want a different life, you must alter that course.

The older you get, the harder change becomes. This is because with age comes responsibilities and duties. With time and with age it also becomes harder to turn to someone like say your parents and ask for help. In fact, they may have left this world. So, it gets more and more difficult with every passing year. Therefore, if you want change, the sooner you start, the better.

If you want change, it must begin with you. You must view the road you're on and the patters that you embraced that got you to this point in time. You must then clearly define where you want to be. Then, you must alter your life patterns to take you on the path towards your desired end-goal. If that means taking classes, take them. If that means mastering a new skill, go and learn it. If that means leaving behind a bad relationship, set about on a path that will consciously guide you away from it. If that means to stop being negative and doing bad things, then STOP IT!

Change is based in a change of your patterns.

What do you ultimately want from your life? What are you willing to do to obtain that end goal? Don't be afraid to alter your patters if change is what you seek.

## What Are You Thinking?

*What are you thinking?*

Few people spend any time considering this. They simply pass through their life, allowing their mind to roam wherever it will, being control by whatever emotion or desire that comes into play. It is for this reason that those on the *Spiritual Path* decide to meditate to find out the source of their thoughts. From this, they come to a unique understanding of SELF and why they do what they do—why they think what they think.

The *Spiritual Path* is not easy. Letting your mind run ramped, that is easy. It takes no control. But, what happens from this lack of control is a wasted life, with no focus or accomplishment.

Every person who has ever achieved anything has done so through a precise sense of focus. And, this has nothing to do with spirituality. It has to do with mental focus. So, if you do not choose to consider yourself spiritual, if you do not choose to walk the *Spiritual Path,* this does not mean that a focused mind will not help you.

In Zen and Yoga the practitioner is trained to silence their mind through meditation. With a silenced mind a very clear perception of life is gained. This is because of the fact that as your thoughts are turned off, you emerge from meditation and see life from a very NEW and clear perspective.

Though meditation is great tool for silencing the mind and coming into contact with the divine self, unless it is taken to the next level it does not reveal the source of your thoughts and why you think what you think. Psychotherapy is a great tool for this, but that requires another person; a therapist. Thus, it is not wholly organic and your conclusions may be influenced by the mind of your therapist.

To get to the source of what you think and why you are thinking it on your own, all you must do is dive deep into your own subconscious. Start by observing what you are thinking right now. Ask yourself, *"What am I thinking?"* Then question, *"Why am I thinking that?"* Once you have an answer, go deeper and question, *"What made me think that way?"* Continue back further and further until you find the source of your thoughts.

This technique is not easy, nor is it for everyone. It requires a desire for mental focus and deep personal understanding that many people do not possess. It is for those who want to focus their lives to the degree that they can succeed at whatever undertaking they proceed towards, while truly coming to an exacting sense of SELF. From this, life is not wasted pursuing meaningless activities that may eventually come back to haunt and hinder your life.

*Get to know yourself!*

## Large or Small

Each of us encounters events in our life that we do not like. Some of these events really make us upset. But, here is the deal... Life, and how you react to it is your choice. You can allow events that you do not like to balloon into large catastrophes, or you can choose to allow them to remain small and inconsequential. It is really your choice.

We each train our mind how to react. As I have long discussed, some people learn very early in their life that if they yell, scream, and throw tantrums long and loud enough, they will eventually get what they want. Many bring this behavior from their childhood into their adulthood and the yelling, the screaming, the throwing of tantrums only gets worse with age. Others grow up more refined. They accept what they are given and move on.

Through the programming we each receive in childhood and through our individualized youthful psychological indoctrination, our personalities are born. But, that is not the endgame. We each can choose to consciously reprogram ourselves to become the person we either want to be or the person we know we should be. We do not have to remain the manifestation of our childhood.

Ultimately, if you allow yourself to blowup due to life events then you have passed control of your life over to those events and the people that have set them in motion. If, on the other hand, you choose to consciously see life events for what they truly are, study their causes, and then consciously move on—you maintain control and you can learn from that particular life situation and understand what you should not do to others.

      Large or Small. Explode or Calm. Who are you? Do you create who you are? Or, do you allow life and the actions of others to dominate your every moment?

## The Near-Death Experience

A lady who stated that she enjoyed my book, *About Peace,* recently contacted me. She explained that she coordinates a group based upon *Near Death Experiences* and she had gotten the feeling by reading my writings that I may have had a *Near Death Experience.* She asked me if I would like to come and speak to her group.

Prior to this, I did not even know that groups of those who had *Near Death Experiences* existed. And, though she seemed like a very nice lady and I am sure her group members were nice as well, I declined.

First of all, for anyone who has read my writings, (particularly read between the lines of my writings), or for those of you who know me—yes, I have had more than one *Near Death Experience.* As I joking proclaim, *"I have knocked on that door more than once."* Not by choice, of course. But, I won't go into those experiences here, as some of them are documented in my other writings.

That being said, I often discuss how our life is shaped by how we define ourselves. We each have a self-image that we wish to project. We each have an individualized mindset that defines our uniqueness. From these factors, we move forward through our life and become either whom we wish to become or who and what society envisions us to be by what we project.

Even though I have, *"Knocked on that door more than once,"* it does not define who I am. Yes, I came away from each of those experiences with new understandings and realizations. But, they are not who I am. Living this life is who I am.

I think we all have heard of people who claim that they can communicate with the dead. Personally, I don't believe it—*dead is dead,* at least in terms of this reality. Seeking to speak with the dead is simply the projections of the living desiring to communicate with loved ones who have passed away that feeds what those individuals claim that they can do. And, there have been countless scam-artists, throughout the centuries, who have profited by claiming that they could do just that; communicate with the dead. They have profited monetarily, psychologically, and physically by tapping into the needs and the desires of those who miss those who have left their physical life.

As I always say, if someone is charging you, don't believe him or her. Knowledge is free!

On the other side of the issue, there are those who, like myself, have come close to death. But, for whatever *karmic* reason, have lived on. Many seek clarifications of their experience. Others seek to compare, to discover if there is one commonality. In either case, what these people are focusing on is, *"Worshiping the experience."*

Now, we all have had unique experiences in our lives. Whether it is a big experience like coming close to death or a little one like falling down and scrapping your knee as a child. From being human, we each have a commonality to those experiences. Yet, due to our own individual psychology we each react somewhat differently to them.

Due to individual psychology and societal programming, in life, there is no one absolute truth. No one way we should behave. No one way we should react. Ultimately, there is no one reality. Nor, is there one answer. We each are as we are. Some people accept this fact while others desire to argue and argue to get people to believe that their understanding is the only understanding. But, as I always say, that is just MIND STUFF.

Here is crux of the issue, *"Life is all perfect."* If you have had a *Near Death Experience* and lived to tell about it, great! If you have not, even better!

We each live our own destiny. We each live what we live. If we are alive, we did not die – even though, (like in my case), a doctor may have said that we did—at least for a certain amount of time.

But, the fact of the matter is, I did not. At least not yet. I am still here. I am writing this.

When you are alive, you are alive! Debating what is on the other side serves no purpose.

**Alive is alive. Live the alive!**

## *Pranayama*

People who study the various forms of *Hatha Yoga* are often introduced to the *yogic* breath control techniques of *pranayama*. *Pranayama* is a method to enhance energy or calm the mind and body by using very specific breathing techniques. This science was developed in ancient times to aid in the practice of meditation and to guide the zealot towards harnessing very specific energies in the body when that specific type of energy was needed for spiritual practice or *sadhana*.

*Pranayama* is an ancient science of breath control but many modern yoga instructors do not truly understand the proper usage and/or appropriate techniques of *pranayama*. Thus, they leave their students with only partial understandings and, in some cases, are actually guiding their students down the road to internal lung damage.

In the modern era, there are many mistakes made when *pranayama* is taught. For example, modern practitioners are often taught to preform *pranayama* indoors, with other students around them. This is not good. There are many toxin indoors, generated by all kinds of things—everything from household cleaners to the chemicals used in the creation of carpets and furniture. All of these things are trapped within the walls of a structure. This is not to mention all the germs each and every person brings into a room with them. As *pranayama* witnesses a person taking in larger amounts of oxygen than normal, practicing inside can actually be very detrimental to a practitioner's health.

This fact aside, many modern yoga instructors may learn the physical techniques of how to perform *pranayama* but they do not understand the subtle elements of the science. This is because of the fact that the practice of *pranayama* has been handed down through so many teachers at this point in history and those who have not studied at its sourcepoint have altered it. From this, the fact of the matter is, the practice of *pranayama* has become very-very convoluted.

Most instructors will argue that they understand the true essence of *pranayama* and that they learned their techniques from someone who truly knows the science. But, as is commonly the case of modern life, this is simply rhetoric.

The fact of the matter is, the best *pranayama* you can do to keep your body safe and your energy cleansed and invigorated is to simply step outside a few times a day and, if the air around you is relatively clean, take in three very deep breaths. *Healthy, deep breaths are the essence of pranayama.*

## In Your Own Moment

Since the dawning of the *New Age* one of the key elements has been, *Getting into the Moment*. Statements such as, *Be Here Now, Get into Your Moment,* and *Feel Your Now,* have been essential key words.

This ideology, and these terms used, are meant to describe a sort of superior consciousness where the individual is feeling some nondescript enhanced since of their life. This is commonly described to the spiritual zealot as something that the average person does not experience which makes it a sought after state of the *spiritual-mind.*

It is common that when the inquiry is made, *"What does getting into the now actually mean?"* Or, *"What does getting into the now feel like?"* It will be described by the pundits as becoming childlike or experiencing everything as if for the first time.

But, what does this mean? And, what are the benefits?

Somehow, in *New Age Spiritual Circles* it has become a type of goal to revert to a childlike mind. A mind of innocence, *naiveté,* and trust. Though, from a certain perspective, this may sound like an ideal quality, there is also another side to this issue. Think about this, these are the same ideological factors that cause the child, and the child-like, to become victims of people and of society. Thus, should they actually be sought after?

But, more important than that, reverting in any way is both an impossibility and an impractical desired end-goal. The reality is, each experience we have lived, each bit of knowledge that we have taken in, has contributed to who we have become. Good or bad, all experiences have made us who we are. To some, these experiences have lead to seeking out a spiritual mindset; which has then guided that person to seek out spiritual teachings which include the concept of, *living in the now.* But, again, what is living in the now? And, how can this be achieved?

From a more refined philosophic perspective, living in the now means embracing each moment as a new moment. Okay. But, don't we all do that anyway?

Let's think about this? *"How are you feeling now?"* The answer is, *"How you are feeling is how you are feeling."* Thus, you are already living in your now.

Many spiritual teachers and spiritual traditions detail that a person should get away from their emotions. They should be removed from them, because they are somehow based in an animalistic level of human consciousness. But, are they?

As human beings, one of the essential components of our make-up is emotion. Thus, emotions are a natural state.

We feel! It is as simple as that.

You can try to hide from emotions. But, they will not go away.

And, no matter how spiritual a person claims to be, they too have emotions. As they are human, there is no way out.

This is one of the big problems when people follow teachers who are no longer alive. A dead teacher is a perfect teacher. Why? Because you will never see or experience their faults or shortcoming. All you will do is to read or hear about their superior consciousness. So basically, all you are exposed to is a lie. Because all living beings have faults, just as they all have emotions.

Now, certain people: the insane, the sociopathic, the selfish, the power hungry, and even some religious practitioners are driven by very negative emotions that are in complete disregard of those around them. They do not care whom they harm to reach their own desired ends. But, these are not the emotions embraced by a normal individual.

Most of us feel happy, sad, embarrassed, frustrated, bored, in love, in anger, and all of the common emotions that are experienced throughout humanity. In terms of, *"The Now,"* these are the emotions that bring us into *the now*.

Think about how much of your life has passed by and you did not even notice it. Every time you ate breakfast, dinner, walked to school, drove to work, and all of the nondescript activity that make up modern life—you lived those moments, but they are gone and forgotten.

Now, think about this, how many dinners do you remember eating when the food was really good or really bad? How many dinners do you remember eating when who you were with made you feel really good or really angry? At those occasions you were brought to an emotional level. Those are the dinners you remember. And, this is just a minor example. Every time your emotions were turned-up, those are the time you truly remember and choose to mentally relive. Those are the times you were truly in your now.

Some *gurus* may tell their students to rebuke emotion and live in a state of placid, meditative abyss. But, what comes from this? A life lived with no memories—as everything experienced is the same. Just as is the case with the boring drive to work, day-after-day, by living life on this level, all life become a blur.

Some teachers say that no emotion and no experience leads to higher-mind. But, does it?

This is one of the ultimate illusion on the *Spiritual Path,* *"Doing nothing leads to something; enlightenment." "A silent mind is nirvana."*

This is all the mumbo-jumbo of teachers who have not lived—teachers who have framed their teachings upon the *Borrowed Knowledge* of those who have walked before them. ...Teachers who want to control their flock and keep them silent and mindless.

Ponder this, one of the key components of Zen is to become Mind-Less. For only there, it is taught, some level of forgotten knowledge is supposed to be lived and experienced. But, all of those who teach this understanding make excuses for why they have not yet personally met *nirvana*.

It is all nonsense. It is all playing to the minds and the wallets of those on the *Spiritual Path*. ...Those who seek some sort of allusive esotericism that can not be had, except only by the most holy. And, who is the most holy? Usually those who are dead or those whom you are not allowed to live with and see their flaws.

Stop believing the illusion. You are living the now, right now!

What you are feeling is your NOW.

When you are hating your job, that is your now.

When you are happy. When you are sad. That is your now.

When you are making your boring drive to work. That is you now.

When you are making love. That is your now.

When you are doing whatever it is you are doing. That is your now.

Stop trying to make, *"The Now,"* some allusive entity that you have to perform spiritual exercises to find. This is your now. What are you going to do with it?

## Things You Will Never Know

The reality of life is that there are many-many things that you will never know or understand.

As human beings, there is the innate desire to understand. *"The how,"* and, *"The why."* Throughout our evolution this has been the cornerstone of both realization and deception.

Realization, because it has caused us to push forward and uncover new realms of knowledge. Deception, because many false-profits have capitalized upon lack of knowledge and have claimed to know things that others do not.

The source of all so-called *Psychics, Mediums,* or *Channels* is that they promise to provide people with knowledge that they wish they had but do not. This can be: *What will happen in the future, What should somebody do next to advance his or her life, Where someone should look for a desired soul-mate.* Or, *What has happened to a person who has died and what are they thinking and feeling from the great beyond.*

In all cases, the answers that are given to these questions are dubious. Why? Because they cannot be proven or disproven. At best, they may bring the questioner a moment of peace and solace or will guide the person to focus their intentions to the degree that they will search hard and long enough until they find what they are looking for within themselves. At worst, they will simply leave the questioning person disillusioned.

But, here is the reality about psychics; *They only exist because people what to know what they do not know.*

As this condition has existed throughout time, psychics, by varying names and titles, have existed since the dawn of man. What they promise is the same thing; *Answers*. But, these answers are not based in truth. They are based in one of two things: *Profit,* because they are charging to give the answers that a person desires. Or, *Control,* because by making an individual believe that they possess their desired answers, the person thereby relinquishes control of their own life. Thus, another person, the psychic, takes control over their reality.

No doubt some psychics actually believe that they have a gift.

As we all have a glimmer of *Divine Consciousness* within us, some falsely believe that they have the ability to tap into this *Universal Knowledge* and do not. The reality is, however, if it is *True Knowledge,* then not only is it freely given but it is never used to control a person. Furthermore, if it is actual *Divine Understanding,* then the person who possesses such knowledge would understand that all, *is as it is*. ...That each person knows what they know. And, are living what they should be living. As such, as all anyone can do is exist in their own perfection, they should never be guided down any path other than what they are already embracing. And, a person's momentary desires would be seen as simply that—*Momentary Desire.* As such, they should never be a motivation for telling someone to veer away from the path of encountering their own perfection—which means, *They know what they know when they know it.* No other knowledge, whether desired or not, is necessary.

Most, *so called,* psychics, however, go to, *"Psychic School,"* for lack of a better term. It is very easy to learn how to manipulate a person by telling them certain things. As certain words and phrases easily guide a person's emotions in a very specific direction. As in all training, the more a psychic does this, the better they become at reading the variations in a person's emotions. Thus, they become masters of control.

This is also the reason most *Psychic Readings* are done in private. In this, usually dark environment, the psychic who has practiced the emotional control over others is allowed uninterrupted control over the mind of their client.

More than simply within the realms of psychic control, religion practices this same theory of domination. Religion, however, practices it over the masses. Think about this, *"How many people have killed and have died in the name of religion?"* A lot! And, they did this believing it was for a just cause; God.

But, more than simply <u>control</u> on a massive scale, religion controls the minds of its followers in much more subtle ways. For example, in Christian churches, after each service, the parishioners are expected to give a donation. They are told this is to help the church. That it is an offering to god. But, what it really does is to finance the lifestyle of the priest or minister. Certainly, in this day and age we have all heard of the bad things that many priest and ministers have been doing to young devotes and the people they desire. So, those donations went to supporting this type of behavior!

Now, a church spokesperson would say, *"No, the money went to the church and those are just isolated incidences."* But, this is not true. Throughout history, the corruption of church official has been well documented, as have been their misdeeds. So, why does the church and/or the various religious denominations still exist? They exist because they promise answers to the people who desire them. They exist because they promise a cure for people who feel that their life is empty and has no meaning. They exist because they offer forgiveness for the perceived sins of the congregation. But, who is the one that told a person that what they were doing was a sin in the first place? It was that same church.

Here is the reality... People want to know what they do not know. They want answers to the questions that they have about life, god, reality, enlightenment, and the ever-after. But, think about it, if you simply accept that life is as it is, then you are free. If you do not peer into knowledge that does not come naturally to you, you are also free. If you do not believe that someone else holds an answer to a question, you are free.

No one else knows anything more than you—even though they may claim that they do. A psychic tells you that they are a psychic so they can make a living—it is their job. They tell you, so they can make money off of you and possible gain control over your life. From this, not only do they gain financial sustenance, they also gain a personal sense of accomplishment and power.

A priest promises answers from a religion that they were programmed into believing. They didn't originate the religion. Thus, it is not based in organic enlightenment. It is simply *Borrowed Knowledge.*

By being a priest, a person gains prestigious and power. They are provided with sustenance by teaching and interpreting borrowed knowledge. If you go to them for advice, they gain power over you. Thus, just as proclaiming themselves to be a psychic, they obtain a sense of personal power.

Again, no one else knows anything more than you! Some may have studied how to manipulate the mind of others. Some may have studied in school or the seminary, so they possess more memorized knowledge than you do. But, they do not KNOW.

Anybody who says they have the answers is lying. Because you are the only person who can know you. You are the only person living your reality. So, there is no one who has the answers for you but you.

## *Interpretation*

People are continually interpreting and evaluating the works, thoughts, ideas, and expressions of other people. ...Interpreting and evaluating in terms of what statement the creator of the work made, what they said, how they said it, what they did or did not do, and what they ultimately meant by it.

Once the initial work in question has been viewed and judged, a person then looks to the creator's other works and then to their life in order to either lend credence to or dismiss what the overall message of what the individual has created. This is especially the case of writings.

Let's think about this of a moment...

People throughout the centuries have written a lot of things. All things written are based upon an individual's personal set of experiences and understandings. Some people truly take the time to analysis life and attempt to come to an understanding about whatever they perceive in this reality. The fact of the matter is, however, most people are not of this inclination. The majority of the world's population is simply locked into whatever momentary reality that they find themselves trapped within—whether it be joyous or tormented. In fact, most people don't care. They simply want to live their life and feel as good as it is possible for them to feel; for a long as it is possible to feel that way.

An individual who bases their Life-Time upon removing as many veils from the illusion of this existence as possible, most probably will find the previously detailed individual's life very wasteful. But, the reality is, that too is a perception; an interpretation.

Any judgment on any person or anything they have created is simply that, a judgment.

Which brings us to an important point. People interpret reality based upon a plethora of cultural indoctrinations, personal experiences, personality-based understandings, and upon a whole lot of other nameless ideologies. The fact of the matter is, one person's reality can never be truly understood by another person. This is especially the case if two individuals lived during different times in history—even if only a generation or two separated those different time periods. For this reason, it virtually completely invalidates the interpreting of the works or the thoughts of another person if the person interpreting them lived in a different time.

**Religious Interpretation**

This brings us to the subject of religious interpretation.

From time immemorial, people have attempted to interpret the words of those that are considered great spiritual teachers. But, let's face facts, Jesus didn't write, *The Bible,* The Buddha didn't write, *The Dhammapada, The Pali Canon,* or any other of the works attributed to his teachings. Other people wrote those texts long after the deaths of these teachers.

Were they exact replications of their words? No, they could not have been.

Moreover, these writings have experienced extensive translations and interpretations long before they ever reached the eyes of those who are reading and reinterpreting them today. By the very logic of this fact, it makes the interpretation of these writing invalid.

Similarly, ancient Chinese texts such as those associate with Kung Fu Tse, *"Confucius,"* have fallen fate to the same process as those experienced in the Christian and Buddhist religions; namely thousands of years of ongoing translations and reinterpretations.

In the case of books such as, *The Tao Te Ching,* it is believed that it was complied by comprising several philosophic teachings and assigning them to one man, Lao Tzu. Whether or not this is the case can never be proven or disproven. Thus, it makes the process of identifying a source impossible.

This being stated, some may wish to believe that the outcome they are reading was inspired by some divine intervention. But, they were, in fact, written by the hands of man. And, man (or woman) is dominated by personal preferences and a desire for things to be expressed and come out in the way in which a particular person or sect desires. Again, the process makes the writing an invalid form of divine truth.

As all of these examples can be assigned to another era and another place in history, where the person who is credited with composing a book never actually wrote it, this then brings us up to the age when an author is actually the author.

With the birth of this time frame, an entire new reality of interpretation of a person's thoughts, ideas, or understandings, has been born. Here/now, reviewers compare the idea(s) of one person to the thoughts and interpretations of another. Today, the thoughts of one thinker may be compared to that of another.

The problem with this style of analysis arises in the fact of the very definition of and for, *Interpretation.* Which is, people enter any subject with a preconceived set of parameters for what they are interpreting. Each person already has a specific belief system before they begin their analysis.

To be fair, each of us encountered thoughts and ideas in our lives that really come to shape us. These may come in the form of words, writings, or philosophic ideals. Wherever these sources of inspiration come from, they shape us and send us on a course that may come define the rest of our lives.

Why do certain philosophies affect different people in different ways? It is simply a case of the human condition. We each are born with a personality; which comes to define what we seek out and who we listen to in life.

This being said, it is these same elemental life-defining ideas that once they are introduced and accepted into our life are the ones that cause us to interpret all additional information from a specific consciousness and point of view. From the point forward where our mind has been shaped, we become set in our ways and base all of our beliefs upon a predetermined set of ideologies.

Certainly, there are some people who are more open minded and accepting than others, but those are the type of people who commonly do not unleash interpretations onto this place we call, *"Life."* For better or for worse, *interpretation* is reality—this is the way of man and woman.

So, what does this mean for you?

One, you can choose to see things in life and accept them for what they are: be they words, writing, art, music, fashion, or whatever. You may not like them. But, you exist in a place of acceptance for those who think and feel differently than you.

Two, you can pass judgment.

Who passes judgment; interpreting the life and works or others? A person who wants to be seen as an intellectual or a knower. Somebody who feels they understand more than the person they are interpreting.

What they are actually doing, however, is passing judgment on another person's works and upon their understandings. And this is the same whether they are criticizing or praising the works of that person or person(s).

Life-Reality is based upon feelings. It is based upon how you feel about a specific subject. How does it make you feel?

This simply equation is what determines whether you will like or dislike anything.

How do you choose what you like or dislike? In many cases it is based on a very superficial level of human consciousness that is determined by what information has been feed into your brain by others. This is why people join religious or philosophic organizations. This is why people believe what they believe. But, there is something much deeper than this. There is a clearer, more perfect reality. A reality where you are not influenced by the interpretations of others. This place in you is, however, very difficult to find. That is the place in you, which is your *True Self*.

That place is where you are who you are. It is *YOU*. Removed are the programmed interpretations of others that have been fed into your brain throughout your lifetime. But, more importantly, it is where you are not interpreting others. Why? Because there is no need for the interpreting of other people thoughts or ideas, because you understand that they are another person's thoughts, another person's realizations; not yours. At this place, you are one with yourself. No interpretation, no explanation is necessary.

*Roller-Girl*

I was in a boutique today. As I was walking around, I noticed that there was another customer in the shop. She was a lady with very long hair. She was probably in her mid-forties. I continued my excursion scanning the store. At one point, I came up next to her. She was looking through the glass wears. I look down at her feet, and she is wearing roller skates. I smiled.

It always makes me smile... In fact, it actually makes me happy when I see someone who truly embraces his or her own style. I mean, most of the world is so busy attempting to fit in that it has become quite a rarity to see someone who really embraces who they are.

I have written about this in the past—discussed how people when they are young are much more frequently willing to express their own inner-vision of themselves and present a true image of a unique style. As time wears on, however, the world takes hold and all semblance of personal style is commonly lost to the hands of time, of age, and of societal integration.

Now, to put this into a frame of reference; it is rare in this day and age that you see anybody wearing roller skates—for even the rollerblading era of the late twentieth century is long gone. This is 2012. But, there she is.

I shopped for a little bit longer. At one point, I see her gliding down the central isle carrying her items, including some of the aforementioned glass pieces. I guess she can skate very well and totally trusts her ability to not trip and fall.

In any case, I get up to the cash register holding the piece of Japanese art that I decided to acquire. She had beat me there but insisted that I go first because she had a large number of items to buy and me, I had only one. *"Love your roller skates,"* I told her. She and the cashier both smiled.

Here is the question you must ask yourself in life. *Do I want to be a unique example of me, not bound by the constraints of normality, or do I want to go unnoticed and blend in?* There is no right or wrong answer. You must simply decide to define yourself by the constraints of your reality.

If you stand outside of the norm, then the world will see you. If you want to be invisible, then you do all that you can to blend in.

It's your life. It's your choice. What reality do you wish to project?

## There is No "Me" in Service

*The reality of life is that most people think about themselves.*

First and foremost, all the majority of the human race cares about is how they feel at a particular moment in time. If they are happy and feeling great, all is good. If they are unhappy, if someone has done something that they do not like then, *Look out!*

This eternal quest for only feeling the way someone wants to feel spans all cultures. Here in the West, due to the pervasiveness of wealth and all-right-ness, it is rampant. The reason for this is that most of the basic needs of life are met. We eat well and we live well. From this, comes one remaining desire to fulfill. That desire is to feel the way we want to feel.

In our current culture most forms of humanity, spirituality, and the desire to truly serve others is the farthest things from the mind of the masses. What is prevalent is, *"I want this!" "I want to feel that way!" "And, if I don't get it, if I don't feel that way, I am going to throw a fit!"*

But, let's think about this for moment, if you are feeling okay, what does that say about the cards you were dealt? That says you are pretty lucky.

When we look around the world there is so much poverty, pain, and suffering; it is hard to fathom. Even in the countries of the western world there is an enormous amount of the same. But, most who are living a life of, *"Okay,"* don't choose to think about these things. They never travel to the places where pain is taking place on a daily basis—even if it is only on the other side of town.

Why? Because most people only care about how they feel in any given moment of time. If that need is being met, then they don't have the time to think about anything or anyone else. Some even question, *"Why should I care?"* Or, they make the excuse, *"There is nothing that I can do about it."*

It is from these perspectives that a person's life is set in motion. A life based in the concept of, *"Me."*

But, in each person's life there comes a time when they are hurt, injured, sick, or completely devastated by a life occurrence. When the, *"Okay,"* goes away; then what?

In most cases, again, all attention is focused on the self. The focus of attempting to get back to the way they were. Again, it is a life based in solely being concerned with the SELF and how that SELF feels.

Certainly, in most forms of religion and spirituality, *"Giving,"* is an essential point. *"Helping others,"* is frequently taught. But, most people don't do this. They may give a few dollars to the collection plate during the service, help with a car wash to raise money for the church, they may even donate some stuff for a bake or yard sale. But, is that giving, in the true sense of the word? No, giving is removing the definition of, *"Me."* It is taking away the component of, *"I feel like doing this."* Or, *"I don't feel like doing that."*

As detailed, each person in their life comes upon a moment when they need help. Most, when they do, they question, *"Why me?"* Some even place all the blame for the life occurrence that brought them to that place on someone or something else. But, here is the actual question that should be asked by each of us when we arrive at those moments, *"What did I do to get here?"*

If you were selfish, spending your life thinking only of yourself; that is your answer.

Most people do not spend any time giving, serving, or taking care of others. Most people spend their Life-Time fighting to get what they want and then when they get it, they spend the rest of their Life-Time fighting to defend it. ...Which is all fine and good if that's what you want your life to be—a constant battle. But, as the old saying goes, *"Live by the sword, die by the sword."* And, dying by the sword is never pretty, painless, or easy.

This brings us to the point that life should not be based upon, *"Me."* It should be based upon, *"What can I do for you?"*

Certainly, people can find all kinds of ways to argue this point. But, on the true path of selfless-service one must remove negative debating from the equitation because all that does is to bring you back to the sense of, *"Me."* Believing what the, *"I,"* wants you to believe. Getting out there and doing nice, positive things is one of the best things you can do with your life. This is not about seeking a reward for it. This is not about seeking a title because of it. It is about doing good things.

Ask yourself, *"What have I done for someone else lately?"* If you have no answer, it is time to change that.

And, these things don't have to be BIG. You don't have to travel to the other side of the world and attempt to save an entire culture. It can all be done in small-steps. Because small-steps leads to the greater good.

For example, if you see some trash on the ground, pick it up. If a piece of clothing has fallen from a hanger in the store, put it back where it belongs. If someone is struggling to carry something, help them. And, so on.

The reality is, at the end of the day, what do we have? All we have is what we have done and given to others. That is the definition of how we will be remembered and what impact we have made on and for the world.

This life is all we know. It is all we have. Do good things in it.

Give. Do good things. Make a positive difference it life. It starts with you.

## *Consciousness Verse Oblivion: Choice Verse Ego*

I went to *Starbucks* this morning. I was standing in line to get my traditional *Grande' Nonfat Latte'* and a bagel.

There were a few people in front of me. Most noticeably there was this one man who was the person directly in front of me in line. He wore the garb of an experienced bike rider: latex shorts and a team jersey. His shoes were the kind that locks into bike pedals on a high-end road bike. So, he obviously had arrived on two wheels.

To put the situation into a bit clearer perspective, the line at this *Starbuck's* leads you right in front of their bakery counter. So, the entire time you are standing in line, you can see what they have to offer.

With that being detailed, the turn came for the bike-riding guy in front of me to place his order. He told them what drink he wanted. Then, he decided to decide what he wanted to eat.

With this, he pushed his way backwards against the line and began studying the pastries and the bake goods that they had to offer. The people behind me began to grumble. Me, I smiled.

I mean, this guy had all of the time he was previously in line to decide what, if anything, he wanted to eat. He chose not to do this but to wait until he was asked.

It wasn't like he was talking to anyone or anything. He was alone in the line.

It took him a few minutes and several changes of mind until he finally made his decision. He was told the price. It was only at that point that he decided to remove his backpack from his shoulders and pull out his wallet from one of the pockets to pay the cashier.

Once this was accomplished, instead of moving out of the way so others could place their order, he set his backpack in front of the cash register and slowly put his wallet away. The cashier rolled her eyes at me. The people behind me continued to grumble. The man slowly did what he did, until it was finally completed. He finally left the cash register.

This is the perfect example of life and how some people choose to interact with it and with others. Some care about the effect that they are having and some do not.

Many people spend their entire life lost in oblivion. Many people spend their entire life lost in ego. Many people think that wherever they are is their space and that others do not exist. It is sad that many people do not care about the affect they have upon other people. How do you live your life?

## The Master

There is a tradition on both the *Spiritual Path* and in the martial arts where a student always pays tribute to their master—the one they learned from. And, there is certainly nothing wrong with this tradition.

But, the key word in this equitation is, *"Student."* As long as you are a student of someone you will always be a student. Some people enjoy this definition and placement in the overall structure of life, because they never have to hold the responsibility. If anything goes wrong they can say, *"Oh, I'm, just a student. The master has all the answers..."*

On the other side of the issue, many teachers also do not want their students to become masters for then they must acknowledge that they have an equal—that they are not the sole holder of the keys to the kingdom.

It is for this reason that it is often stated by teachers that they have not passed on all of their knowledge to any one student—that they have kept a certain amount of it to themselves. From this, those on the outside, those students of lower rank and understanding, will believe that even a senior student is not a full master—not a true knower.

The reality is, the teacher who behaves in this manner is basing their teaching upon ego—*I know and you do not.* But, is this the true way to pass on knowledge? Is this the true way a teacher should behave?

From a martial art perspective, I have long understood and commonly discussed that, yes, a teacher does guide you into mastery of the physical techniques of a particular system of self-defense. And, though in the early stages of training they show you how to properly deploy offensive and defensive movements and they correct your techniques. But then, it is you who must come to understand how your particular body operates and what movements your body and mind are most ideally suited to employee. Knowing the answer to this question is personal mastery. As each person's body is different. And, each person has a unique understanding of physical interaction—be it physical combat or otherwise, the master in you arises when you move away from performing solely what you were trained to do and emerge with your own unique understanding of physical self.

This is true of the relationship between the spiritual teacher and the student, as well. Though the techniques of spirituality: be they meditation, *pranayama, hatha yoga,* spiritual dance, or whatever, are more mentally refined than many of the physical techniques performed in the martial arts, they are none-the-less taught to you by a teacher and then it is you who must make them valid; must make them real. You must understand their source, calculated by your own being and then integrate them into your own personal psyche for those techniques to lead you to their end-goal of self-realization.

Therefore, though we each initially enter into a *dojo* or a meditation class in order to refine our body and mind to emerge as a better, more whole and complete person, we must kept in mind that we should never be held back by the instructor.

Enlightenment is you. It is in you. It can become you. Physical and mental mastery is in you. It can become you. But, you must understand you will never embrace ultimate knowledge if you remain a disciple, a student. It can only occur when you allow your mind to process all that has been taught to you and then you emerge with your own truth, your own understanding of how the world, the universe, and god operates through you.

First of all, you must be willing to allow that knowledge to come. To do this, you must be willing to move from the realm of a student. Once it does arrive, you must allow it to be as unique of an understanding as you are a person. This is the ultimate secret to obtaining enlightenment. There is no ONE enlightenment. It is a unique as you are.

## Life Happens in a Second

I was sitting out on my patio this evening. It is thankfully very cool here in California this mid-July. With a glass of *pinot noir,* (on the rocks), in my hand, I stared out across the Pacific Ocean. The colors were those of the perfect painting—grey and blue fading into one another.

The grey marine layer etched the sky in its cloud-like substances and merged to the grey blue of the ocean far off in the distance. Light from the remaining elements of the sun pieced the veil and allowed in minor glimpses of yellow and orange in the sky.

I was looking out to this island in the distance. One of the California Channel Islands. *Santa Barbara Island,* I believe. I was realizing that though I have viewed it many-many times, I will probably never get to travel to its shores. So close and yet so far...

As I sat studying the hues, a hummingbird comes directly into my field of vision. He (or she) stationed themselves just a few feet in front me. For a moment, it hovered there. Then, it flew away.

In that moment, I saw all the perfection of life. The beauty, the essence...

After the hummingbird had flown away, I had to thank it for stopping by.

...For giving me that moment of art and perfection.

In life, there is all the, *"All That..."* All you do. All the time of life wasted in all the doing. All the thinking about what is to come and what has proceeded in the past. All the what you should have done back when. All the what you will do in the up-and-coming future. But then, there are those few moments in each of our lives that we are reminded that life happened in a second and that perfection is unleashed by the most unexpected circumstance and situations.

This is the essence of *Satori*. This is the manifestation of *Nirvana* in life.

## Sins of the Father

Some people have a very good childhood. They grow up with a supportive family and passed through adolescences into adulthood with support, guidance, and positivity. Many of us did not have that luxury, however. We grew up in what would now be defined as, *dysfunctional families*. When we did something that our parents considered wrong we were punished by being hit with belts and other objects, in association with being verbally abused.

When we think of the biblical reference, *"Sins of the father,"* (Exodus 20:5, Exodus 34:6-7, and Deuteronomy 5:9), our minds commonly go to something to the effect of that a child takes on the *karma* of the parents. But, it is much more simple than all that. Each of us is a product of our upbringing and how our parents behaved when we were growing up. Like the old saying goes, *"You are what you eat."*

From our earliest moments forward, we are trained how to behave and how to interact with life by how our parents acted. If they were kind, intelligent, and thoughtful, that is the type of person we more than likely became. If, on the other hand, they were mean and abusive, then that is most probably what we became.

This is a very easy equitation to process. Simply look at a person's childhood who has walked down the wrong road in life, and you will find all of the answers to why they have done so by viewing their upbringing and their parents.

A situation that clearly illustrates this evolution comes to mind. I know this one family where the boy is now twenty years old. When he was young, he was one of those super smart kids that everyone thought would really make something of his life. But, his father was an arrogant jerk, who lived off the money of his parents, did nothing with his life, and was just not a nice person. Then, one evening in a fit of rage, he blew his own brains out in front of his wife with his son in the other room. Think about how that would affect a child's evolution?

A couple of years later this boy OD'd and stroked-out. He was only eighteen years old. He had linked up with the wrong crew of people and was doing wrong things, including some hardcore drugs. His life was barely saved and when he returned home, he could not even remember how to climb into bed. That is how bad his stroke was. Time has passed and the boy has seemingly recovered. But now, at twenty, he stands in family photos flashing gang signs. Gone is the hope for his pathway to success. All that is left is to hope that he will not hurt himself or someone else.

Now, that is a very extreme example. But, perhaps even more important to this story is when we look back to the, *"Sins,"* or *the karma* of his more expansive family. For example, the grandmother did some very bad and extremely selfish things to her daughter, (the mother of the boy), and to other family members. Previous to the detailed set of occurrences, I occasionally wondered if her *karma* was ever going to come into play. Well, not only did the detailed situation occur with her grandson but other negative events appeared in her life. So, parental behavior affected more than one generation.

Most examples of, *"Sins of the father,"* are not as extreme as the previously detailed case. That being stated, many of the people who are in jail, gang-banging, committing crimes, and doing bad things have come from parents and/or a family that has walked a negative life path before them. Not everyone, but for many... And, this is their foundation into badness.

There are two levels here that each individual must look at as they move their way through life. *"The sins of the father,"* can be overcome. It may not be easy. You may have to fight against what you know and how you have been trained to live and behave. But, it can be done. Also, if you are a parent, you really need to decide to change any negative training you may have learned from your parents. I have seen so many of my contemporaries simply mimic the way they were raised. And, as such, they interact with their children through fear and violence. So, if you are a parent or may become a parent you have to get off of the

*Zombie Treadmill* and reprogram yourself to be better—to be more than the parents who raised you. From this, *"The sins of the father,"* will be nullified.

## Things You Will Never Know

On the *Spiritual Path* there is a propensity to find out, *"The reason why."* To lift the veil of illusion and come to know, *"The reason for."*

In many ways, this is the ultimate essence of the *Spiritual Path*. To come to know the illusive, the mystical, and the unknown.

In fact, in all levels of life there are spiritual practices assigned to explore the depths of human action and human experience.

Think about this... The first thoughts the mind goes to when one thinks about spiritual practice or *sadhana* are actions like meditation. But, from the dawn of advancing human consciousness forward, these spiritual practices have expanded and have moved onto becoming practices that define the more mundane practice of life. They now encompass the way one gardens, performs a tea ceremony, onto physical combat, and even sex. It is not that this makes any of these physical actions any more or less worldly, it simply makes them a new way to refine human consciousness.

And ultimately, isn't that what the *Spiritual Path* is all about? Refining your consciousness and bringing even the mundane acts of life into the realms of the spiritual?

It is for this reason, particularly in this modern age, that those who walk upon the *Spiritual Path* attempt to investigate each and every aspect of life in order to come to a new, unique, and more aware conclusion about what is actually taking place in this place we call, *"Life."*

An interesting experienced happened to me today, which illustrated, at least to my mind, how we each seek to know—how we what to know the essence of even the things that do not matter that much.

I was driving North on the 405 freeway here in Los Angeles. There was a lot of traffic as the late morning promises. The traffic in my lane had stopped but the traffic in the lane to my left continued to move. I noticed a motorcycle policeman driving in that lane. What made me take notice of him was that the color of his uniform and his motorcycle were not the colors used by the L.A.P.D. or the California Highway Patrol. As I was attempting to gain a look at his motorcycle or his uniform patches—just at that moment, his lane stopped and mine began to move. So, I could not make anything out.

As I continued to drive North, I could see him in my rear-view mirror, but I could not make out the lettering on his motorcycle. Then, in a flash, again he drove past me. I tried to read his police department logo, and I thought it read, Buelton.

For those of you who may not know, Buelton is a town about one-hundred and fifty miles North of Los Angeles, located along Highway 101. The town is perhaps most famous for a restaurant that serves pea soup.

From my early childhood forward I have never been found of peas soup, though I have eaten at that pea soup restaurant from time-to-time. Eating something other than their peas soup, of course.

None-the-less, my most memorable thoughts of Buelton are of its *McDonalds,* which is right off of the freeway. From the 1980s forward, on my many trips up and down the coast, I frequently stop there for a large coffee from their drive-through window and occasionally I also get a hot fudge sundae.

In any case, though I thought I saw Buelton on the motorcycle logo, I could not believe my eyes. Why would a motorcycle cop from a community so far north be traveling solo on his motorcycle in Los Angeles?

I thought through all of the local communities that started with the letter, *"B,"* but I couldn't come up with an appropriate answer to sooth my questioning mind.

I realized this is like so many elements of life and particularly spirituality. Things come to your mind, and you wonder... Ideologies pass you by which makes you question... But ultimately, there is never an answer. It is simply what you ascertain it to be.

Though I had come to terms with the fact that I would probably never know where the motorcycle officer was actually from, his lane eventually stopped, and I pulled right up next to him. Yes, he was from Buelton!

Then came the question, *"Why?"* Again, it is so many miles from Los Angeles, why would he be down here, in his full uniform, riding a city issued motorcycle?

Though my first level of questioning came to be answered, the next level of inquire would and could never be.

This is the ultimate statement of seeking answers on the *Spiritual Path*. You seek, you inquire, and some things you come to be understand. But ultimately, life and the reasons for, remain a mystery. They remain lost to the unknown.

And, this is part of the ultimate understanding that each of us must come to embrace on the *Spiritual Path*. There will always be questions remaining. Though some may claim to have all of the answers, they do not. All they have is what you have; the ability to uncover a few of the mysteries of life.

You may have beliefs. You may have faith. And, those are both fine. But, do not confuse your beliefs and your faith with fact. For fact is based upon an entirely different set of perimeters that can ever be expressed on the *Spiritual Path*.

Ultimately, this is the greatest element of the *Spiritual Path,* it provides you with a reason to explore levels of life and existence that most people never even think about. But ultimately, those of us who walk upon the *Spiritual Path* come to understand, *we don't know everything.* And, That's great! That's what keeps life a mystery. Keeps it interesting. Keeps us exploring the new realms of understanding and consciousness.

## How People Craft Their Life

I always find it interesting how people set a pattern for their life.

I have discussed this fact many times in many different ways. I have also talked about how everything a person does and does not choose to do is, at least partially, based upon their culture and how, and with whom, they were raised.

This being said, at the end of the day, we each decide to make choices that set the course of our lives in motion.

I think back to an amusing story that happened to me when I was seventeen. By that point in my life I was fully engulfed on the *Spiritual Path.* I was very closely linked to the *Sufi Order* and the *Sufi Dances,* formalized by Murshid Samuel L. Lewis, which later became known as, *The Dances of Universal Peace.*

In any case, by that point in my seventeen year old life I was the one who collected the $2.00 entrance fee from each person as they entered the dances on Tuesday nights.

Though most of the people who attended the dances on a weekly basis where what could be called, *"Regulars,"* frequently there were new faces in attendance, as well.

One of the things that commonly set these, *"New faces,"* apart from the rest of the crew was how they were dressed. Most of the regulars wore what could be termed, *"Spiritual garb."* At least, *"Spiritual garb,"* for the mid 1970s. Meaning, the men commonly wore drawstring pants and a *kurta,* (an India style shirt), while the women wore long flowing skirts and *kurta* style tops. *Malas* or pray beads were, of course, quite common. And, the overall vibe was very depictive of the spirituality of that era.

One night a girl walked in. She was obviously new. I had never seen her before. She wore what may be best described as a grey wool business style skirt and a blouse. She had long dark hair and was very pretty. We immediately made a *first-glance* connection. She paid her $2.00, went inside, and the dances eventually commenced.

I was very drawn to her. So, at the mid-dance interlude I went up to speak with her, asked her name, etcetera. After the dances that evening, I again went up to her and suggested we get together. She used the word, *"Later..."* I smiled and that was the end of that evening.
The next day, I was back at Hollywood High School and she was off doing whatever she was doing...

The next week's dances rolled around and the girl reappeared, paid her $2.00, and went inside. This week, however, at the interlude, she came up to me and suggested that we meet up later in the week. The plans were set.

Me, the terrible student that I was, took time off of school at every opportunity... So, when the midday time of the meet appeared, I happily arrived.

We met one cloudy Los Angeles afternoon. I drove to her apartment that was not far from where I lived. Her apartment was north of Franklin Avenue and west of Western Avenue in the Hollywood foothills. I lived just south of Hollywood Boulevard and east of Western Avenue. It is amazing how just a few blocks totally changes the socioeconomic make-up of a neighbor in a city like Los Angeles.

The day, the date if you will, went along fine. We got back to her place and she told me her story. And, I am paraphrasing here... Her boyfriend had moved out the week before and now she needed a new man in her life. I guess, I was the chosen one.

She made the decision. A decision that I had nothing to do with. But, I smiled to myself. She didn't even know me. But, she had made up her mind. I was the one to move in.

Now if we look at this from a psychological and even spiritual perspective, it is quite interesting. Here is a pretty girl, she lives in a nice apartment in a good part of town. But, she is incomplete without a man in her life.

Speaking of a man... Her last boyfriend had just moved out but there was no grieving, no heartbreak, no teary eyes, just, *"You're next;"* referring to me.

I found that very strange. Certainly, there are a lot of roommate situations based solely upon convenience and the need to share the price of the rent. But, here I was being promised, *"Love."*

Now, we could go into the fact that, particularly in times gone past, there were a lot of arranged marriage and the like. But, there we were in the modern world. And, this is L.A. She wasn't just offering me sex. She was inviting me into her life. And, I guess she assumed that she was such a package that I would drop whatever else I was doing, wherever else I was living, and immediately come and live with her.

Certainly, in the mind of the worldly adolescent that I was, the thought did cross my mind to throw it all away and move in with her. But, I turned her offer down. At that time in my life, my eyes were set on going to India.

So, let me just say, it didn't work out: the her and the I. I mean, though I may have appeared to be something and someone, as I was the money-taker at the *Sufi Dances,* the reality was, I was still in high school.

You see, this is the thing about life; what we decide to do, what choices we decide to make, sets not only the next segment of our life into motion but also the entire rest of our life into motion. What we do today determines the choices we will have tomorrow.

The fact of the matter is, though you can throw blame to everything and on everybody, it does not even matter what previous life-events led you to the place you find yourself today. Whatever you do from this moment forward should be based upon the understanding that what you do today, leads to who you are tomorrow. For this reason, any decision you make, no matter how rapidly you must make it, should be based upon your desired end-goal for your tomorrow and the rest of your life.

I don't know, maybe the girl experienced, *"Love at first sight,"* with me? But, if so, she didn't pursuit it. And, even for the 1970s, it was kind of unusual to immediately ask a person to move in—a person that she did not even really know...

The point of all this is that life is your choice. I keep saying this and saying this. But, I am continually contacted by people asking me what they should do when they believe that they have made a faulty choice in their life. What I always say is, *"Think about your life. What do you want? What do you want your tomorrow to be? And, what are you doing today, to equal that end result?"*

Ultimately, there is one thing in life that you must understand, *every other person is different than you.* They want what they want. If they want you, then the two of you can spend time together. Maybe a lifetime. But, they are not you. You must define who you are, what you want, and what choices you are willing make to get to what you want. If the two of you find a common ground, great! If not—*the two of you are not.*

It is essential to understand that you cannot possess someone. Just because you want somebody does not mean that you can have him or her.

Physical and material things you can save up for and/or visualize into your life. Things are not people. Though everything possesses energy, the energy of, *"Things,"* is much easier to harness than that of a person. It for this reason that if others are involved in any life equitation, it all gets convoluted by individual desires. To this end, if you focus your energy on the haveable, the doable, the achievable, then life becomes so much easier.

If you make your choices with a focus upon the end-goal then you can define your life and you will not look back wishing you had made, *"Better choices."*

## Life is Defined by Availability

I have long discussed the fact that life is defined by availability. What this means is that your life is defined by what you have available to you. Whether this is people, money, culture, language, beauty, size, shape, learning opportunities, friends, family, or whatever... That available is what ultimate makes you who and what you are.

Some people are very good at pushing their availabilities to the maximum level. You see this in people who come from literally nothing and rise to the top of their profession, climb up the social and economic ladder, move to new and better locations, and so on. Many times, these are the people who are revered and even commonly referenced in the statement, *"If they can do it, so can I."* But, in reality, this is not the case. Whatever it was that gave them the ability to rise to the top was set in motion by their set of availability. Meaning, it was a combination of personality, desire, drive, plus who and what they knew.

But, it is essential to note, what they have or had is not what you have or had. This is not to say that taking advantage of your particular set of availabilities is a bad thing. But, you cannot define yourself by what others have achieved. Moreover, you should not judge yourself or be hard on yourself due to what others have achieved and you have not. Because if you are behaving in this manner, what you have set up is a mindset of self-deprecation, which only leads to a low opinion of self. From this, all kinds of negative life elements are born.

This being said, lack of life availability can also be seen as the one factor that holds each of us back from achieving our dreams. Lack of life availability is the ultimate demon of actualization.

This is because of the fact that we are each a creature that embraces desire. Through our culture, through the time period in which we live, and through all the desires that we are told we are supposed to have; desire is the common point of all human life.

Our families tell us what they hope we will become. Our friends guide and share our desires as per our specific socioeconomic and cultural environment. And we, in the quiet of our own minds, focus on the dreams we hope to achieve.

Now, in terms of spirituality, it is commonly taught to, *"Let go of desire."* And, this isn't a bad ideology. But, it is much harder than the words proclaim.

Desire is the defining factor of life. With this as a basis, you can either choose to live a life defined by desires—attempting to get everything that you want, which will make you live a life continually defined by gain and loss—leading to a constant state of un-peace. Or, you can choose to desire no desire. Each time a desire arises in your mind, you can beat it down. In both cases, though they arise from differing sides of the spectrum, you are still defined by desire.

Life is lived by availability. You are born, you are educated, and you are surrounded by a specific culture—all framed by a specific point in history. Within that framework you are provided with a very unique and specific set of circumstances. From this, you decide which desires you allow to rises. You decide what you want. Once you have decided what you want, defined by your family, your friends, and your culture, you will then decide to either pursuit it or decided that you can never have it. In either case, what you do next will set the next group of availabilities into motion in your life.

Most people do nothing. They do not try. They give up before they begin. Or, they try for a moment, decide it is too hard, and quit. This is not bad or good; it is simply a defining factor and a condition of life.

Others try and try. But, the sad truth is, they try for something that is unhavebable. For example, many go after relationships with people who do not want to be in a relationship with them. And, this is just bad. It haunts both of the lives and no good ever comes from it.

Ask, receive a, *"Yes,"* or a *"No,"* and move on.

In other cases, people go after careers that they were just not meant to possess. Many want stardom. They want to be on the silver screen. Or, they want to have their music heard across the globe. And, these are just two examples that are common here in the twenties-first century.

A few generations ago, these careers would not be a source of desire at all. In a few generations forward, they will probably fall by the wayside. And, these are just a couple of examples.

The fact of the matter is, people don't want small things. They want it, *"All."* They go to all these lengths to get that, *"All."* But, what does that, *"All,"* mean? You don't know, because you are not there. You only think that you know.

Every life situation is completely different than expected. Every life situation you live changes you forever.

Relationships go bad. Then you don't want them anymore. You're sorry you ever got involved.

Jobs and careers each take their toll on your body, your mind, and your spirituality—no matter how seemingly great they appear from the distance.

The primary problem is, if you spend your life in purist, all you are left with is that pursuit. If you no not achieve it, you will be sad and unfulfilled. If you do achieve it and it is not what you thought it would be, you will be sad and unfulfilled. But, the reality is, in either case, this is life, what you do is what you do. What you live is ultimately what you live.

Your life is here for only a moment. Then, it is gone.

You are given a specific set of life availabilities. Maybe it is *karma*, a gift of god, a blessing or a cure. But, the availabilities you are given are what you are given. Each step you take in life provides you with a new set of availabilities. In those availabilities you must choose who you are and what you will do with them.

You are given availabilities. Your life is lived by availability. What do you choose to do with them?

## *Why Do You Believe?*

Why do you believe what you believe? It is a simple question, but most people do not have an answer for it. In fact, most people do not even question why they believe what they believe. They simply assume that is the way it is. In other case, people will fight you tooth and nail to tell you what they believe is right. But, if you demand an explanation of why they believe what they believe, all they can give you is that it is written, that is what Jesus, Mohammed, Buddha, or some other profit spoke and they have faith in those words.

Now, I won't even go into the fact here that virtually any religious book, that was written over a thousand years ago, has gone through so many revamps and retranslations that the original words were probably lost long ago. I won't go into that, because that is not the point. Nor will I go into the point that we are all products of our family and our culture. For again, though that is very true, it is not the point. The question remains, *"Why do you believe what you believe?"*

In the 1960s and into the earlier part of the 1970s, when there was a *Consciousness Revolution* taking place, some people would say words to the effect, *"You are so programmed!"* Or, *"You have a lot of your mother in you..."* Each, referring to the fact that people were simply spouting information that they had been taught in their childhood and had never moved onto their own definition of reality. The problem is, with statements such as these, the person who was saying them was simply attempting to exude their own intellectual superiority in an attempt to get someone else to buy into their own personal belief system.

But, where did they come upon that knowledge? In most cases it was simply either directly from some other teacher or a conglomeration of what was being postulated at the moment among a specific spiritual circle.

The fact of the matter is, all levels and all definitions of heightened consciousness have already been detailed. If not in writing, then in speech or in the mind of some other individual who has walked the face of this earth. So, what does that tell you?

With this, we come back to the question, *"Why do you believe what you believe?"*

In reality, if you are on the path of consciousness, it is essentially important that you have an answer to that question. It is also essentially important to understand that there is no one right or wrong answer. No one can tell why you believe what you believe.

In churches, temples, synagogues, mosques, and the like, you are told what you should believe, how you should believe, and why you should believe. But, these avocations come from a person. A person who is as flawed as the rest of us, even though they may hold the title of Priest, Minister, Rabbi, or Murshid.

And, for some, (most in fact), what someone in that position says is enough to set, *"Belief,"* in motion. Is that enough for you?

On the path of consciousness, we must ultimately remove as many layers of illusion from our life as possible if we hope to merge with supreme knowledge. To achieve this the first thing we must do is to question everything. For by questioning, answers are revealed.

It is important to note, we may not like some of the answers that we find. We may not like that from self-inquiry we have revealed illusions that we may have preferred remained unrevealed. But, this is the path of conscious; this is the spiritual path. We must break through all levels of presupposed knowledge, revealing who we truly are, what we truly believe, and what we are destined to become.

## *I'm Glad You Received Your Karma for What You Did But How Does That Help Me?*

As I've been involved with Eastern Mysticism for virtually my entire life, the subject and the study of *karma* has often been brought up as a source-point of conversation. I've written several pieces on this subject and spoken on it often. And, I can tell you, if there is one thing that everybody across the globe thinks about, no matter what religion they come from, it is the subject of *karma*.

Now, I am not going to go into the fact that I believe most people really do not understand the subtle levels of *karma*. But, I will say, *think about it before you really try to apply it as a Life-Science, because it I complicated.*

That being said, I believe that each of us who has been wronged by somebody thinks, (either out loud or to ourselves), *"Just wait. You'll get yours..."* And, generally people who are selfishly motivated or do bad things have their *karma* catch up with them. That's just the way life works.

Now, once again, I could go into all kinds of discourse about who or what is actually wrong—because, (in many, if not most cases), good or bad is only a point of view. But, I think we can all agree that BAD is beyond just what one person thinks it is. BAD is done by someone who is only thinking about themselves and not caring about the effect or the affect they are having on others. For example, stealing something is BAD. Hurting someone is BAD. Breaking someone's something is BAD.

Killing someone or something is BAD. And, no matter what your motivation or excuse for doing what you do, we can all agree that certain things are agreed upon as BAD.

So, we get to the central subject of this discourse. That person did something BAD. They got what was coming to them. But, then what? Yeah, they may be hurting from receiving their *karma*. But, did them getting hurt give you back what was stolen from you? Did it replace what you lost? Did it fix what was broken in your life? Probably not. Maybe it strokes your ego or your intellect to think, *"They got theirs."* But, does that make your life any better? At best, that is simply Mind-Stuff. It does not take you back in time and fix what that person took from your life.

This is the whole thing about *karma,* (and the misinterpretation thereof), people may get what's coming to them but that doesn't fix what they broke?

## *You Hold All of These Things in Your Mind*

One of the primary facts of life is, *you hold all kinds of things in your mind.* Meaning, we all hear things, read things, and are told things. Whether or not these things are actually factual and/or true is unknown. But, due to the fact that we learned of them, they retain a space in our mind.

Think about this for a moment; how many stories have you read or been told throughout your life about people, about situations, and even about events in the course of human evolution and history? When you are told these stories you either instantly dismiss them as nonsense, if that is what they seem to be, or you place them in the portion of your mind as, *"Deemed believable."*

There is one absolute truth to life, however, and that is that people lie. Some people lie to make themselves seem better or appear to be more than what they are. Some people lie to cover up evens that they wish would have occurred differently or had a different outcome. Some people lie to make another person look bad. No matter what the cause, no matter what the logic, no matter what the reasoning, the fact is, people lie.

The fact that people lie should alter each of our perceptions of reality. Why? Because we hear the untruth and not knowing that it is untruth we base our perception of a person or a situation upon what we were told. If it was a lie, what are we believing?

The other side of this issue is that people repeat what they hear or read. If they have been handed an untruth, they may propagate this untruth with no ill intent. They simply heard a fact that they considered to be interesting or true and then continued to spread the falsehood through their circle of friends. From there it may spread to larger and larger groups. It then has the potential to spread all across humanity.

Right or wrong, this is simply life. This is part of the human condition. It is what makes up our life-understandings.

Now, if we had the inclination, we could research every element of every world we hear or read. But, that would be so time consuming that there would be no time to live our lives. So, in essence, there is no way around the life condition of hearing falsehoods.

I believe that most of us have had at least one situation in our life where we heard and/or read something and believed it to be true. Then, somewhere down the road we hear a more correct interpretation of what actually is the truth and we either become amused at ourselves for buying into the falsehood or actually become angry with ourselves for believing the lie. But, at the end of the day there is nothing that we can do about it. We heard what we heard. We believed what we believed.

This subject matter should not send us into a state of overall distrust or a cynical approach to all people and all writings. What it should do is cause us to understand that life is lived by perception. It is defined by what each of us desires to occur. And, we each have separate and differing desired outcomes from life. By understanding yours, you will be able to know that ultimately life is an illusion; this physical plane is full of all kinds of untruths. Some are man-made, while others are set in motion by cultural, religious, or political ignorance.

All we can ultimately do is exist in our own space, our own perfection, as to each of our lives will come a multitude of untruths. This is simply reality.

What we must personally attempt to do is to never propagate untruths simply for the sake of words spoken or written in the meaningless pursuit of self-embellishment; *i.e., I know something but you do not...*

Live your life as simply as possible. Which, admittedly, is complicated in this modern world. But, by embracing the perfection of simplicity you will not be led down the wrong road by untruths spoken by others. In addition, by not spreading the untruths spoken by others you will not be adding to this less than spiritual element of the human condition.

## *Your Own Agenda*

Have you ever noticed that sometimes when you communicate with people you will be thinking that you are discussing one subject but then a little bit farther into the conversation you realize that the person you are conversing with was saying what they were saying from a completely different mindset—they were talking about a completely different subject than you believed the two of you were discussing?

The reality is of life is people have their own agenda. They want what they want from life and from you. Thus, they are choosing to interact with you for a very specific reason.

In some cases, human interaction is not all that contrived. You meet people at school, at work, and you are forced to deal with them within the confines of those environments. You may like them, you may not like them, but you get along—you do what you do and then you leave that specific environment and go on to where you go on to. In the workplace, some of the relationships last for years-upon-years but you give them little thought.

Those relationships are easy. They are defined. It is when you take the next step and move towards an actual chosen interactive relationship with an individual that things become complicated.

When you meet someone and you make the decision to interact with him or her on a personal basis, what is your motivation? Why did you decide to befriend them? For the most part, you saw something in them that you liked. Maybe it was their personality, maybe it was their looks, maybe you felt you could gain something by being friends with them. Whatever it was, there was a reason, a logic that you decided to move the relationship forward.

As the old saying goes, *"It takes two to tango."* When you begin to intact with a person, they too must be involved in the exchange.

Now, here is where it gets complicated. ...Why they are participating in the relationship may be completely different from the reason you are. What they want may be completely different from what you want.

Though this may all sound very logical. How many times have you begun a personal interaction only to find out that the person you were dealing with was on a completely different page than you? They wanted something from you that you could not give. They want to gain something from you that you either did not have to offer or were not willing to give.

In your case, maybe only wanted to make contact on a friendly level. But, what later occurred was nothing that you expected.

In life, there is no way around this. People are people.

Churches and religious sects will tell only to associate with those of your same congregation. From this, you would expect that those people would have the same mind as you. But, this is not the case. Though you may possess the same core beliefs, every person is different—every person wants something slightly different from life and from the personal relationship in their life. So, no matter where you meet a person, even if you hail from the same sourcepoint, you are not them and they are not you. They have their own agenda.

What this tells us about life is that wherever we go you must keep this fact in mind. Though most people are nice, they are nonetheless motivated by their own set of perimeters; they have their own agenda. They want what they want.

On a bit more subtle level, understating that people want what they want is simply part of the human condition. Most people want what they want, but if you don't want it too, they are fine with it. But, people come at you from all angles. Some forcefully want what they want and they could care less about the consequences. Others are much more subtle—much more calculating. They will try to study your thoughts and your expressions in an attempt to shape your actions. This is called, manipulation. Others, will take your words, restructure them, and use them against you. This is called, deceit.

Ultimately, most people are so locked into their own mind and guided by their own set of desires that they do not even realize, or in some cases care, what they are doing. They are doing what they are doing to gain what they want. They have an agenda.

Each person has an agenda. The reality of life is that you may not understand another person's agenda until you have succumbed to it or been damaged by it. For this reason, though you cannot and should not go through life with a sense of mistrust, you should go through life with an understanding of the flaws of humanity. People want what they want from you. They want what they want from life. All people, have an agenda.

## *Meditation is Everywhere*

Traditionally, a practitioner of meditation is taught to remove themselves from all external sights and sounds. Most forms of meditation teach the meditator to close their eyes and ignore all sounds that they may hear. Personally, I have long believed that meditation is everywhere. Instead of running away and forcing yourself to pretend to not hear sounds, you should embrace them and make them part of your meditation.

Most people now live in urban environments. In the cities there is a constant barrage of sounds. Not only are there the sounds of nature, such as wind, rain, birds and the like, but there are also all the sound of man: cars, airplanes, construction, and people talking.

Attempting to turn your mind off and not hear those sounds is very difficult. This is especially the case for the individual who is new to meditation. They sit down and they try and try to not be distracted, but the sounds take them away from their meditative mindset. Then, as they have become distracted, their mind finds its way to think—thinking about all the things the mind likes to think about...

But, if you take a different path of meditation; if you allow the sounds to become part of the process, then meditation becomes much more natural.

For example, when you initially S*it,* it is always a good idea to calm your mind with a calming breathing exercise in order to gain a *Center* and a refined sense of control over the *Self.* Once you have done this, you can allow your mind to become focused. Then, instead of running away from your environment, embrace it. If a car drives by remain focused. Instead of becoming distracted by the sound, follow its sound as it drives off into the distance. If someone is pulling their suitcase or bag on wheels, listen to it rumble across the pavement. If you hear a lawnmower in the distance, allow its motorized rhythm to capture your mind and hold it fixed. If you hear a siren, embrace its sound; study it, come to understand its essence, as you listen to it fade off into the distance.

In both urban and country environments there are the sounds of nature. The sounds possesses in nature tend to be much more constant and soothing than those of the city. But, they can be none-the-less no less jarring to a meditative mindset if you try to turn your ears off from hearing their sounds. So again, when you sit to meditate and you hear the sounds of birds chirping, wind blowing, ocean waves crashing, or a river flowing; instead of attempting to hide your mind from it, embrace it. Allow it to become a part of your meditation. Let the sound guide you deep into the overall essence of nature. Become a part of it. Understand and embrace it.

Being what you are, where you are, who you are, while fully taking in and merging with the sourcepoint of the energy that is surrounding you is the ultimate form of meditation.

*Higher Consciousness:
A Study in Fiction*

Since the dawning of advancing human understanding, people have put forth the fact that you can advance your consciousness, you can become more, superior, even enlightened. At the core of all of these teachings is separation. By seeking higher consciousness you are becoming more than the person next to you. They are of a lower mind because all they think about is their desires, their car, their house, their family, their whatever... But you, the seeker; you are more! You are something different – someone more holy because you are on the path to higher consciousness.

This trend, this definition, has been taught a thousand different way throughout the various religion traditions and spiritual schools across the centuries. There have been a few teachers who have stepped to the forefront of the pack and have expounded new and somewhat different teachings. And, for whatever *karmic* reasoning, they have been remembered throughout history.

Schools and religions have been created around their name: Siddhartha Gautama, *the Sakyamuni Buddha,* Jesus, Mohammed, Sri Shankaracharya, and so on. Then, there have been the teachers who reference these individuals as supreme beings. Many of these teachers devote their entire lives to, *The Becoming,* of what those teachers propagated and the higher consciousness they were believed to have possessed.

But, let's step back here for a moment. *"What is higher consciousness?"* What do you define it as? What do your teachers tell you it is?

The first step in understanding higher consciousness is defining what it is to you. Because what it is to you, may not be what it is to me.

The next question you must ask yourself is, *"Does pursuing higher consciousness actually make you something more, something better as has been laid down throughout time?"*

No one can tell you the answer to that question. I can say, that if we look at the masses of humanity, we can affirm that most people pursue nothing more than the fulfillment of their momentary desires. They want what they want. But, then you must realize this—they want what they want, just as I want what I want, and you want what you want. ...Just as the person seeking higher consciousness wants what they want; namely, higher consciousness.

Ask yourself, *"Is the pursuit of higher consciousness any different from wanting a new car, a new girlfriend, a different boyfriend, a new watch, or whatever?"*

Certainly, there is the belief that a person on the *Spiritual Path* is not so much seeking things only for themselves but are more set upon a course which is designed to aid in the betterment of all of humanity. For example, there is the *Bodhisattva Vow* where a person makes a vow to gain enlightenment for the benefit of all sentient beings and once they have achieved enlightenment they will continue to reincarnate, (continue to come back to this place we call life), until all of humanity is fully enlightened. That sounds great. But, is it?

If we take a more refined look at this concept, it brings us back to the primary point, *"What is the key concept in the Bodhisattva Vow?"* It is that one person will do one thing. They have heard of it. They desire it. So, they pursuit it.

Though the spiritual practitioner may make it sound like they are doing something for the good of humanity, we still come back to the central focal point of, *"I." "I will do this. I will get that. Then, I will do this for you to make all things better."* Me, me, me…

Can there be any concept of, *"Me,"* or, *"I,"* in true higher consciousness?

Some spiritual traditions teach that their techniques cause a person to lose all sense of, *"I."* But, this is one of the main selling points that has been used in the propagation of the use of hallucinogenic drugs, *"You will lose yourself. You will become one with all"* But, this is all *mumbo-jumbo*. It is simply a means and a method to convincing people that there is some strange and illusive *Cosmic Thing* out there that they cannot encounter naturally.

To the matter of the fact; yes, some hallucinogenic drugs will cause you to lose your sense of Self. But, then the drug fades and you are back where you were. The only problem is, the drug has altered the chemistry of your brain forever and you are never the same. And, that, *"Never the same,"* is not a good thing. Or, the drug has altered your brain to the degree that you become mentally ill. Today, there are now some pharmacological drugs that can help reverse this pattern. But, nonetheless, you will be left with, *"Never the same."*

If we look at this ideology a bit deeper, *"What do you become if you have no sense of self?"*

Again, here we go into the rhetoric of higher consciousness. It is often stated that, *"This person's consciousness is so high that they are completely removed from self and are completely removed from this world."* So is a person who is insane. Are they enlightened? Have the achieved higher consciousness? Immediately the argument will be made that they did not choose their condition, but a holy man did.

But, you must realize that choice is a condition of life. We all choose what we choose. And, for the most part, people who want to be something, oftentimes pretend that they are just that even if they are not.

Some will exclaim, *"Oh no, my guru isn't like that!"* How do you know?

Most people never have the opportunity to spend enough one-on-one time with their teacher to truly see that they have human flaws. They are simply allowed to see a presented image. Moreover, if one follows one of the, *"Supreme teachers,"* then all ability to see who they truly were is long lost, as they died a long-long time ago.

All of this is not to say that there is not spirituality. And, this is not to say that there are not those who truly pursue higher consciousness. But, how many times have you found yourself thinking, *"Oh that teacher is a fraud. He or she is not truly holy."* How many people have said that about your teacher or about you?

As there is no one definition, there can be no one higher consciousness. Since there is no one higher consciousness, like all things it life, its pursuit is left to the definition and the belief system of the individual mind. What you believe may be completely disavowed by the person sitting next to you. And, in fact, a few years down the road, you too may completely believe something different than you do today. Belief is only that; belief. It is a perception individually held by each person. It is not universal. As it is not universal there is no one to attainment. There is only YOU and what YOU believe.

What do you believe and why?
What do you desire and why?

## God's Job

When people pray, they all ask god for the similar things. *"Please give me more money, a better life, a new relationship, a child, a new job, a new chance; please let me move to a new city/a new country; please give me my health back, please let me be young again, please let me defeat my enemy."* Even, *"Please let me find enlightenment."*
Though the words are the different, the desire is the same. When people pray, they want more.

Wanting more is a condition of life. This is because of the fact that people are universally dissatisfied with what they have. Some more than others...

Some may be happy with certain elements of their life but virtually no one is happy with everything.

So, god is continually bombarded with requests.

Religion has made up all kinds of excuses for why all of these requests are not met. *"God is testing you..."* Or, *"You are not ready to have that desires fulfilled as of yet..."* And the list goes on.

People also explain to themselves why their prayers are not answered. *"I am not worthy." "It is just my karma." "I am being repaid for something I did wrong in the past." "I'm a sinner." "I am cursed." "God doesn't love me." "God never listens to people like me." "I haven't prayed or gone to church for so long, god has forgotten me."* Again, the list goes on and on.

For every desire, there is a reason for a desire. For every unfulfilled desire, there is a reason for its lack of fulfillment.

People turn to god, when they are not able to actualize what they want to come into their life. This is not good or bad; this is simply the way it is.

God is the last resort on the path to life achievement.

Some people are very religiously devout and they make the worship of god the primary focus of their life. They go to their church all the time. They pray for the benefit of others and the betterment of the world.

But, desiring anything different than it already exists is based upon one causation factor; desire. Desire for things to be different.

Again, god is deluged with requests.

All requests made to god are based in unfulfilled desire.

From a metaphysical standpoint and perspective one can say, *"Let go of all desires and you are free."* Yes, that is true. But, that is not the reality of life. People desire. Thus, they contact god.

But, who is god and what is his job.

By virtually all definitions, god is the all-pervasive overseer of everything. He, (or she or it), is the source of everything. Thus, by that very definition, it would not matter how many people are making requests—as god is all-pervasive so the number of requests would not bog him down. And, as god is all-pervasive and all-knowing, he does not judge. So, your desire should be met. That's his job. Right? Giving his creations what they need.

Now, here comes the tricky part. What do you really want?

A lot of people may think they want this or that, but what are they willing to do to achieve it?

We all want what we want!

Think about this... What did you want when you were a child of say ten years old? Did you get it? Do you still want it now?
What did you want a year ago or even a month ago? Do you still want it now? And, what steps have to taken in achieving it?

Life is based on momentary desires. Most things we want until we don't want them anymore. Maybe we get them and no longer desire them. They weren't what we expected them to be. Maybe we did receive them, and we simply got bored with them. In other cases, we lost interest. Or, our desires changed.

How many things have you desired and at some point you stopped desiring them and the thought of them completely fell away? In many cases, you do not even remember your desire.

Ultimately, life is lived. We live then we die. That's the human condition.

During that time of life, we all want what we want. Most, never truly try to achieve their desire(s). They may pray to god to get something, (as that is the easiest way), but then the desire fades and it is forgotten. People give up on its achievement before they even try.

So, is god doing his job? Probably. Are you?

## The Birth of Karma

When most people think of *karma,* they think about the person who has done something very bad and will be paid back someday or the really good person who is given some sort of blessing for doing the right thing. But, *karma* is much more subtle that.

The story: A new neighbor moved into my building next-door to me. I briefly met him. He seemed like a nice enough guy.

As so many people these days, including myself, predominately work from home, I came to find that he set up shop right next to the wall of my dinning area. There he began to talk and talk for hours upon hours on the phone.

As my computer system was set up to the side of my living room, when I would sit down to do my business all I could hear was this guy going on and on and on about whatever he was discussing on the telephone. His ramblings drove me nuts.

I was reminded of the old Paul Simon song, *Apartment House Blues,* *"On man's ceiling is another man's floor..."*

In any case, at first I tried wearing my shooting range headphone. But, after a half hour or so they really begin to bother me. I would take them off, *"Wow no talking!"* I was elated. I tried to get back to work. But, then I could hear his phone ringing, *"Hello..."*

Finally, after a few days of these on-goings, I realized I had no choice. I would have to relocate my workstation if I hoped to get anything done.

With this realization, I disconnect all of my wires, remove my computers, monitors, scanners, printers, and speakers from their placement and pulled my desk into the bedroom; where I re-set up everything. Obviously, this took a lot of time.

In the process, I hear something hit the floor. I turn around and look, and my printer had taken a dive. Why? I don't know. But, it did. It was broken. There was nothing I could do to change that fact.

Then, once I was re-set up, I pull out the keyboard drawer from my desk. Snap, tiny ball-bearings go flying onto the floor. Something had happened in the move. The keyboard draw had dislodged and broken loose. Even though my desk is over ten years old, that does not mean that I don't like it. In fact, I like it a lot! So, I was a bit unhappy.

From all of this move, brought on by another person, I will have to replace my printer and either fix or replace my desk.

Now, let's get back to the main point of this piece; *karma.*

Did my new neighbor do anything wrong? No, not at all. I couldn't complain to him or the management for he was just being who he is. If he had a dog that barked, was partying late into the night, or if he was playing music loudly; then maybe. But, he is only living. So, there was nothing I could do or say.

This being said, his actions did, none-the-less, set *karma* in motion. Him being who he is—his actions resulted in necessary reactions on my part. I had to move my work area. In the process my printer and my desk were damaged which caused me to have to take additional actions to replace or repair them; which costs money, which equals the necessity of more actions.

You see, this is life. We all interact. For the most part, we never even take the time to think how our actions, how what we are doing, will subtly affect others. This is especially the case if we are walking the *Spiritual Path* and attempting to do right by the world.

Everything we do affects others.

Thing about how the things you never even think about are affecting others.

*Karma* is very-very subtle.

## What Happens When It Doesn't Work?

I was coming across the border from Tijuana into the States. Sometimes the border crossings get really crowded and you sit in bogged down traffic for a long-long time. There was a guy in a car next to me. His car was overheating. You could tell he was obviously very upset about this. But, being in this long line to the boarder what could he do? Finally, he purchased a Mother Mary statute from one of the roadside venders—obviously hoping to gain her *grace* to make it across the border. For a while he continued to inch forward. Finally, his car gave out. It completely overheated. He got out and pushed it through the traffic over to the side of the road in Mexico.

How many times have you done something in order make things better? And, I am not discussing taking a positive physical action in order to make something different. I am asking how many times have you turned to the spirit world via either a picture, a statue, an alter, a whatever, in order to hopefully make things in your life better? Maybe you've turned to *Feng Shui* or something like that…

Now, in some cases when you bring spiritually based physical objects into your life or rearrange the physical objects you have, things do get better. At least for a moment. *"Wow, it worked!"* But, what about when the good you desired does not last forever? Then what? A new spiritual object? Maybe one with more promised power?

In most cases, like the guy in the car, a physical object, no matter how seemingly holy, does nothing to change anything. Is that the fault of the object or is that the fault of you for expecting an object to do anything?

Religion and spirituality makes all kinds of vague promises. When these promises are not met, then religion and spirituality provides all kinds of excuses. *"I was not deserving." "I am not pure enough."* And, so on... But, physicality is not true spirituality. True spiritually is accepting what is here, now—even if you don't like it and then dealing with it in an appropriate manner.

Save your money. Instead of buying a god to worship, use the money to fix your radiator.

## *Control IT or IT Controls You*

Life is full of temptations. They come at you from all directions. Desire, of course, is the big one. Desire for love, desire for sex, desire for money, power, fame, whatever… Then, there are the more subtle temptations—those introduced by culture, family, friends, or advertising. These are things like smoking, alcohol, drugs, and even food. Each of these has the potential to possess very bad implications.

Not only does smoking smell bad and invade the space of those who do not smoke, but it can kill you. I have watched people die from lung cancer caused by smoking and believe me; it is a horrible way to die. Yet, people continue to smoke, invading the space and the health of others, while guiding themselves down the road to a very bad death.

Alcohol, we all know what that can do to a person and the devastating effect a drunk driver can have on the lives of other people. Yet, alcohol is one of the most common components of modern culture. But, alcohol kills! It kills others and it slowly kills the abusive consumer. And drugs… We all know about the devastating effect drugs have on the life of the person who becomes addicted to them and the people around that person. Yet, they are very prevalent throughout the world, and a lot of people take them.

Then we get to food. Food is a necessary component of life, yet it is abused just the same as the previously mentioned items. People get fat. They are unhealthy. They hate themselves for being fat and wish they were not fat. They become very negative people and do negative things because they have low self-esteem due to their weight. Yet, they make excuses for being fat and they continue to drink bad drinks, eat bad food, and continue to grow.

In many cases, these intoxicants, (and food is included in this list), are, in fact, encouraged by friends and family. That does make it right. But, this is life. That is just the way it is.

But... We need to look at ALL this from a different perspective. We need to see how these, *"Things,"* can become educational elements of our life if we interact with them from a different perspective.

When I was studying *Tantra Yoga* in Khajuraho, India it was taught that all things, all elements of the *Spiritual Path,* are about control; Control IT instead of IT controlling you. And, this is very profound if you think about it. Because in terms of desire, drugs, alcohol, and even food, so many people allow those THINGS to control them, instead of being in control of them.

Many people assume drugs are bad. And yes, they can be very bad. Yet, people take them. In fact, throughout India, people—some of them actual *sadhus,* will try to give them to you. This is based in the fact that in India, just as with the American Indians and some other cultures, certain drugs are used in order to give the taker a glimpse of higher consciousness. In these cases, instead of simply using them as a way to get high and/or feel better about life, they are used as a pathway to Self-Realization. In these cases, the mind of the user is not gear towards letting the drug take control. Instead, the mind of the participant is in control, and it guides itself towards a clearer, higher mind.

Now, I am not suggesting anyone take drugs to find enlightenment—because most people do not possess this mindset or the discipline for this. What I am saying is that, in these cases, a person who uses them for this purpose is in control. Thus, it does not lead them down the road to addiction.

This is the same with something as simple as food. Food tastes good. It is fun to eat. Yet, food can make you fat, unhealthy, and miserable.

An amusing sidebar here… In the mid 1990s I decided I wanted to gain weight. I had been skinny my whole life, and I decided it was time for a change. So, I ate a lot more. Hanging out with this one friend of mine aided this process because he ate a lot. The only problem was, he had a hiatal hernia. So, he would often throw up halfway through many of the meals we ate—in restaurants or wherever. That was pretty gross. But, none-the-less via hanging out with him, I did put on thirty pounds.

Due to the fact I was and am a very active person and I was running four miles a day; it was very hard for me to keep the weight on. I realize this is the opposite of most people who gain weight. But, the point is, my weight gain happened due to my control over it, not its control over me. And, when I decided I didn't want the weight anymore, I choose to lose it. And, I did.

The moral of the story is, you have to be in control of your life. If you are not in control, you have to take control. You have to get focused and do not let your desires, your intoxicants, or even your diet control you. From this, not only do you make an exciting impact on your life, but also you also come to feel the power of personal control over your life. From this, you can move deeper into your own spirituality or into any other area of your life you hope to gain access to.

      Controlling and manipulating others is easy. Controlling yourself is much more difficult. Be in control of yourself.

## Buying Into Their Own B.S.

As I have often detailed, for whatever *karmic* reason, I have walked the *Spiritual Path* for most of my life. And, I use the term, *"Spiritual Path,"* for lack of a better term. But, I am referring to those of us who have decided to make the evolution of human consciousness and tuning into and understanding the *Great-Beyond* their primary focus.

As someone who has been on this road for a lot of years, I have witnessed many things about people on the path. Perhaps most disconcerting is those who buy into their own bullshit. But, I'll get into that in a moment...

People are drawn to spirituality for an untold number of reasons. Some enter the path at a young age, and some enter it much later. Most, when they decided to, *"Get Spiritual,"* find their pathway in organized religion— which is very pervasive and universally accepted in all cultures. So, it is easily at hand. Then, there are the more abstract realms of spiritually which call out to people like me. In either case, the person who has newly found the path is generally the most fervent about it.

I remember when I was a young boy of about eleven or twelve and I was sent to summer camp. One of my camp-mates was a young boy who used to love to make flavored toothpicks and chew on them. He brought his little bottle of liquid cinnamon spice, and he would daily dip a few toothpicks into it to keep in his mouth throughout the day. Though this seemed a bit strange and bizarre to me, what was more curious about the boy was that he had already decided what he wanted to do with his life. He was going to be a minister. While most children of this age group have little idea of what they want to become, he had decided. Me, I wanted to grow up and be like Neil Young or Jimi Hendrix. In any case, he had set upon his path very early in life. Whether or not he ever became a minister, I don't know. But, what I do know is that youth who enter the *Spiritual Path* possess a deep belief in the possibilities of what it has to offer. In fact, this is not only true for youth but for others who enter the path at whatever stage of their life.

Once upon the path, the first-step is generally to seek out a teacher to guide you down the road to your ultimate end-goal. This is where the problems begin. I have seen it so many times. A person new to the path is full of anticipation, promises, and belief. Thus, they are quick to believe whatever they hear and are easily taken advantage of.

The reality is, when a person is new to the path they are full of exuberance. Belief equals exuberance. But, what comes next?

In this state of exuberance many desires to go out and spread this emotion to the world. They want others to be as full of joy as they are. Me too... When I was young, I wanted to tell all my friends and family about what I was experiencing and guide them to experience the same. This, even though most people do not desire to walk down this road.

As time progresses, however, and a person's knowledge becomes deeper, they generally no longer need to go out and spill their spirituality onto people who are not of the same mindset and do not desire to walk down the path. They simply become who they are and embrace their cosmic understandings in a more pure and personal space.

But then, there are the others... Those, who as they get older, decided that they have something unique to give; they have found their calling. They believe that they possess something—a deeper knowledge that others do not hold. Thus, they decide to become teachers. From this, they move forward to spouting out the same recycled spiritual rhetoric that has been handed down since the dawning of advancing human consciousness. And, oh yeah, this usually equals them getting paid for what they teach or, at least, being provided with other various favors.

In formalized religious, there are generally schools that a person must attend to rise to the level of a teacher. On the *Spiritual Path,* this is generally not the case. So, anybody can go out there and claim that they have had a particular revelatory experienced and that experience is what makes them so all-knowing and the one that other people should follow. But, their experience is generally not real. It is simply something that they have read about; something that they have projected as something deep and meaningful, or simply they have realized this is a good way to attract people to follow them to feed their pocketbooks and their ego.

Mostly, what I have seen is that the people who do this spout knowledge that they have read from books written by other people or have heard at lectures. But, whatever it is, their teachings are based upon what I call, *"Borrowed knowledge."* It does not rise from a pure, personal source—though they will, of course, argue that this is not the case till the end of their days. But, the truth is the truth. These are the people who buy into their own bullshit. They believe they are something more than others—that they have something to offer, something to teach.

Spirituality is an organic, uniquely individual, space of consciousness. Even though two people may be following the same teachings, their interpretation and internal understandings are uniquely their own. People believe they need a teacher because people seek interaction, and they seek affirmation that what they are thinking is okay. But, is what you are thinking, what you are thinking? Or, have you been guided to think that way?

This is the ultimate understanding of consciousness. Are you, you? Or, are you the creation of someone else's belief system?

Being you, you are free. That is *nirvana*. Being what someone else tells you to be is *maya*. That is illusion.

Here are a couple of simply rules so you don't step into someone else's bullshit:

1. Have you heard what they are saying before; from another source? Perhaps said in a slightly different way?

2. Are they charging you for their knowledge? Knowledge is free. It doesn't cost a dime.

3. Are they calling you, *"My child, my loved-one, my dear-one?"* If they are, they are projecting that they are more than you. No one is more than you. You are the source of your own spirituality and enlightenment. Be you! Not a student of someone who buys into their own bullshit.

## Sometimes You Have to Adapt

In each of our lives things are going to occur that we do not desire. Situations are going to happen that we do not want to happen. People are going to be around us that either disturb us or do things that bother or actually harm us. This is just the way it is.

We are not getting what we want, people are not behaving the way that we want, and thus, these life-actions, that we did not ask for, cause our reaction which can equal frustration, anger, and even depression.

Certainly, when possible, we can address the issue and try to change our circumstances. But, often times, the things that are happening to us are out of our control. And, if we confront the people who we believe are not behaving correctly, all that is equaled is a confrontation that may lead to further crisis.

The only answer is to adapt to the human terrain. Meaning, instead of fighting, instead of being is a constant state of frustration, anger, or depression; move, change your mental landscape, change your mindset.

For at the root of any life-dissatisfaction is you. You may be right. You may be wrong. But, in essence, the right or wrong does not even matter, because it is only you who is being affected by the life-situations that are surrounding you.

You care. No one else cares. Even if others pretend to care, they don't really care. That is to say, they don't care unless it is affecting them, as well.

In the martial arts, I teach my students that if one technique is not working against an opponent, do not lock yourself into that technique; do not continue attempting to try make something work, when it is not working—because if you follow this path all you do is waste your energy. Instead: adapt, change, and keep moving until you find an approach that does work.

If you are being bothered—physically move away, if you can. If you can't, mentally move away. Be willing to adapt in life, get away from what is bothering you.

And, the main thing, don't seek it out. Once it is there and you know it is there, mentally let it go. Don't reread the book because all that does is to cause your mind to be forced to relive that which you do not want to live in the first place.

Adapt. Let go. Don't let the rude, the obtrusive, the mind-less, the arrogant, or the negative, control you.

## *Why Don't You Take the Time to Actually Achieve Something in Your Life?*

Each generation has its own unique signature for its time on earth. For this generation, it is the Internet.

Personally, I witness the Internet come into existence. And, I was one of the first people to actually jump on the *World Wide Web* long before it was ever called that. The moment it came into existence, I immediately understood its benefits, and I quickly began to see its problems.

One of the main dilemmas I immediately noticed was no longer where you are interacting with a person face-to-face. No longer did you know whom (or what) you were talking to. People simply became screen names. They became unchecked fact expounders. They became people who claimed to be something that they were not. In other words, deception became the norm.

Certainly, many people express whom they truly are when they are on the Internet. Many, however, do not. They do this for an untold number of reasons. Mostly, I have found if someone hides behind falsities on the Internet it is due to the fact that they are not secure with who they are and what they have achieved. The Internet provides them with a perfect vehicle to become their own fantasy.

Good or bad, this is just the way it is.

The other thing I have witness, which is perhaps even more perplexing, is that many of those people who have created an Internet persona for themselves, often do this by basing what they say or do on the names, the fame, and the works of other people. For example, search a famous person's name. What will most commonly come up is initially that person's biography. Then, what you will be presented with is what some other person thinks, feels, or writes about that famous person. From this, someone who had nothing to do with the development of this person's research, creativity, or fame has been etched to the annals of Internet notoriety by simply detailing what they think or have decided about a known person.

This is also true with other elements of life, as well. On the Internet people who have little or no training can instantly become experts on anything. They do this by simply claiming to be an expert. From this, all kinds of physical, psychological, and spiritual tragedies have occurred.

The biggest problem I find with the Internet is that people no longer have to achieve. They simply can become something by claiming that is what they are. They have no credentials, no schooling, no anything... All they possess is a desire to be something more than what they truly are.

For example, to write about a person in times gone past one generally needed a degree in journalism or a similar subject. If they did not possess this, the established news services or publishing houses would not publish their writings. To discuss history, psychology, health, or whatever, one previously needed an advanced degree in the subject. If they did not possess this degree, they would not be allowed to write or to speak on the subject. From this, truth in publishing was held to a much higher standard than it is today.

Now, in this age of the Internet, anybody can write or say anything; whether it is true or not. They can jump on the fame developed by another person and instantly gain notoriety for themselves simply by discussing that famous individual. They can start blogging or entering statements on a public website about a subject they have never studied in school or mastered in life. Yet, simply by taking the time to write a few words they are somehow/someway viewed as an expert. But, they are not! They are simply someone who has not personally achieved anything and are simply jumping onto the bandwagon of someone who has.

What has occurred from all of this is that people no longer achieve. What they have become is individuals who would rather stay on the Internet and have their words read by the masses, but they never developed the true foundational ability to actually speak with authority on the subject. They could not go to a university and teach the topic, because they do not possess the advanced degree necessary to do so. They could not go in front of a group of established individuals, who have excelled in their field and speak, because they do not hold the credential necessary to be accepted. Yet, on the Internet, they can write anything; and claim themselves to be right.

The Internet generation has been given a passageway to not truly achieve. Yet, they hold in their hands the means to claim or write anything.

Each generation is given a blessing and a curse. In this case, the Internet is both.

Each person has to individually decide how they will use the tools of their generation and how what they do with these tools will affect their own life and the lives of those to come.

## Positive or Negative

We live in a world of positive or negative. Some call this *Yin and Yang.* By whatever title you give it, you are either doing things that create positive energy, or you are doing things that create negative energy.

Positive and negative is, in certain ways, defined by personal perspective or by what team you are on. But, at the end of the day, no matter what your personal ideologies may be, it becomes very evident if you are doing something positive or if you are doing negative.

How can you tell? Simply look at the results.

Some have questioned, *"What does it matter if I do something positive or if I do something negative?"* The answer to this can only be based upon your own interpretation of reality and what you want your mark on this world to be.

If you do and say positive things, positive results occur. If you do and say negative things, negative results occur. As you are the source of either of these energies, then you are the one that will ultimately pay the price for what you have unleashed.

Whether you believe in *karma* or not is unimportant. The fact of the matter is, what you say ultimately affects you. What you do ultimately affects you.

Why? Because what you say and do has an effect upon other people. As such, what you say and do comes back to you—because what you say and do will set a course of events in motion around you and cause the people you interact with to behave in a certain manner. Thus, whatever you instigate will ultimate come back to you.

Most people don't think about this. They think they can say or do anything and as long as they get away with it, they will remain immune from the consequences. Though your words and your action may not come back to haunt you immediately; good propagates good, bad propagates bad, and ultimately you will reencounter what you have unleashed.

For example, you're doing something positive equals positive words and positive actions performed by other people creating an atmosphere of positivity. This occurs based upon what you have instigated. This is the same for doing something negative. Doing something negative creates an atmosphere of negative words and deeds.

Does what you have said or done equal a deluge of negative words and actions? Or, does what you have done and said equal an atmosphere of positivity?

Negativity is a very easy drug to become dependent upon. This is due to the fact that negativity causes your adrenalin to flow, your heart rate to go up; which leads you to a state of excitement. Negativity is also addictive in that once you have found that you can cause other people to rise up, this provides you with a sense of misguided power and control. But, the ultimate fact of the matter is, this type of energy has no benefit to the betterment of the world and will only come back to damage your personal evolution in the long run.

To find a motivation to embrace the positive over the negative, simply look at an elderly person who has embraced a life of negativity. What has their life become and how happy and fulfilled are they?

Some people want to argue the fact that what they are doing is actually positive; when, in fact, it is very negative. Some people desire to justify their actions in order to give themselves a rationalization for the continued adrenal flow they gain through embracing negativity and from inciting others through negativity. In fact, some people are so self-involved that they believe anything that they are doing is right and never take the time to truly study the consequences of their actions.

People love to come up with justifications for doing whatever it is they are doing. This is part of the human condition. It does not make it right. It simply makes it part of the human condition.

Positive or Negative; the ultimate definition is based upon the effect you are having on others and how what you are doing is aiding in the betterment of the world.

The fact of the matter is, many people don't care. They only think about themselves; how they are feeling and how their team is behaving. This is why the world is in the condition it is in with so much conflict.

The conscious person, on the other hand, attempts to make all things calmer, better, and more positive. Though it is impossible to always succeed; that is their goal. That is what they work towards.

What is your goal? The answer to that will give you the definition for who you are and if you should, (maybe), think about changing.

## Karma Heavy People

I believe that each of us has witness somebody who has done bad things in life and we have thought, *"I wonder when they are going to receive their karma?"* Most of the time we do not continue associating with an individual who we feel is not living a good and/or positive life, so we separate from them and never know what happens to them latter down the road. In other cases, for whatever reason, we see a person later in their life and we see that they truly are being hit hard by what they have previously done—that they are, in fact, receiving their *karma*.

This is one of the strangest places to be in life. For, on one hand, you understand that the person deserves whatever *karma* they may be receiving. On the other hand, it is hard not to feel sympathy for what they are going through.

The reality of life is, most people have family and friends that walk with them through their existence. In doing so, they too get hit by the *karma* of what a specific person has previously unleashed.

Here lies one of the perplexing questions of life, *"Does only the person who has unleashed the negative deeds suffer the karma or are other individuals dragged into the melodrama simply for doing what a family member or a friend is expected to do; stay close and help?"*

One could philosophize about this question for eternity. And no one answer could ever be found. What can be known is that no matter what your relationship to a person is, you will be encompassed by the energy of the company you keep. Bad or good; energy is energy and whom you choose to associate with will affect your life.

There may be a million justifications for why you are associating with a particular individual. *"They're my family." They're my friend." "I'm in love with them." They were there when I needed them." "I hate this person for ruining my life. So, I am here to get back at them and make them pay for what they did."* A million reasons... But, life is an ultimately a choice.

We all live. We all do what we do. We are all judged by others. And, this is an important point. People judge people. They decide that they like or dislike an individual. They decide if they approve of or disapprove of their actions. They do all this from personal perspective. But, this mindset is not what sets *karma* in motion. What a person thinks about you is not a *karma* creator. In fact, just because somebody may not like you or your actions is not what creates *karma*. *Karma* is created by how you treat people and life in association with you.

If you do things to people solely to make your own life better, that is a *karma* creator. If you do things to people and do not care about the results you are having on other people, that is a *karma* creator.

At the end of the day, what you do, how you live your life, will create your *karma*. And, you will experience the repercussions. Plus, those close to you will also feel them, as well.

The sad reality is, most people are so locked into their own mind that even if their *karma* is spilling over onto someone else, they don't realize it. As an outsider, you may see it. But, a selfish, self-motivated person rarely can pull their self away from thinking only about themselves long even to even witness what they have brought to the life of another person.

You will see this all the time. People will say, *"Sorry but there is nothing I can do."* Or, when it is happening to them, they scream, *"Why god?"* But, they never seek the source.

This is part of the human condition. People create *karma*. They only care about themselves. And, when what they have done does affect someone else, they do not even understand their own responsibility in the matter or simply make excuses that they are not personally responsible.

The answer? There is none. This is life. This is where we live. All we can do is be as good as we can be—associate with the best people we can. And, if we must associate with a *karma-heavy* person, we must keep our spiritual guard up so the negativity they have unleashed in times gone past does not catch up with them and take us down in their sphere of energy.

## *The Meditative Pathway to Insanity*

There is a meditation technique that is taught where a person initially focuses their attention on their inner-mind and then they begin to separate their mind from their body and raise their I-Consciousness above their body. They are taught to intentionally move their mind above their body and begin to view themselves as if they were seeing themselves through someone else's eyes. After they have practiced this meditation technique for a time, they are then instructed to move this technique forward and cause their mind to move farther and farther away from their body, eventually and hopefully interacting with the cosmic realms of the universe.

This meditation technique is named different things by the different schools that teach it. I believe it might be best titled, *"The Meditative Pathway to Insanity."*

The reason I say this is simple. Meditation is a practice designed to cause the body and mind to enter into a state of profound harmony. From this vantage point the higher realms of consciousness may be experienced. The previously described technique, which is also used in Astral Projection, is designed to separate the mind from the body. Of the people I have known who have encountered mental illness due to meditation, this technique was the primary cause.

Thankfully, psychiatric science has vastly moved forward in recent years, and many doctors have been schooled in how to deal with this type of self-imposed body-mind separation that creates a rift in the human consciousness. This combined with the fact that there have been a number of new drugs developed in recent years to counteract this level of altered consciousness and, as such, they provide people with a way back to reality.

For anyone who has ever experimented with mind-altering drugs such as LSD or Psychedelic Mushrooms, this same level of body/mind separation is a byproduct of that drug experiences. But, as the drug wears off, so does the experience. When people push their minds into this level of consciousness, via meditation, the effect may not wear off—in some cases forever.

Some people believe that simply because they are being lead through various meditation techniques by a teacher, they will be safe. This is not the case. There are many self-proclaimed teachers of meditation out there. Though they may believe in what they are teaching, they may not possess the necessary training to properly guide their students to first understand how to maintain a tether to their physical form or how to properly bring themselves back to focused human consciousness if their grasp on reality is lost.

As I have long said, *"In India, the crazier you are, the holier you are."* That being the case, crazy is not an applicable means for interacting with everyday reality, even if you are walking on the *Spiritual Path*.

For this reason, I believe that the ultimate meditation causes you to be conscious and then holy from a place of here-ness, from the space of in this body-ness. Meditation should not be a method to

alter your mind to the degree that you will not be able to be a part of reality.
    Think before you meditate.

## Why a Guru is Bad

We all have had teachers in our lives. Some of them have been very influential and have caused us to become the people we hoped we would be.

Certainly, all of the classes we took in school helped us grow as thinking individuals. Though we may not have liked all of our classes, they each caused our levels of understanding and intelligence to increase.

There is another side to education, however. That is the education we seek out and gain once we have entered the *Spiritual Path.* Here, however, being taught and learning becomes a very different field of reality.

In religion and spirituality you are no longer being taught elements that are designed to make your life more functional. You have stepped beyond reading, writing, and arithmetic. At this level you have entered the realm of supposition and dogma. At this level, someone who claims to hold knowledge of the more abstract realms of reality is the one who is teaching you.

But, do they truly hold this knowledge? Does anyone?

When you are being schooled in generalized scholastics, the answer to two plus two becomes self-evident. But, in the realms of spirituality there is no such thing as fact; there is simply belief. And, many people confuse belief as fact.

When you go to a spiritual teacher you are expecting to be guided down a road that will lead you to self-realization and/or communion with god. This is what you are generally promised by the teacher. *Do this, do that, and you will end up here.*

But, there is a very big problem with this; people are only people. Though they may truly believe what they are teaching, that does not mean that they truly possess the inner-knowledge of what they propagate. This is where the big problem with spiritual teachers begins.

I cannot tell you how many supposed gurus I have met over the years who have been telling everyone how to live. But, they were a complete mess when no one was looking. Though they may have even believed what they were saying, they never learned how to truly embrace the essence of what they were teaching. Yet, they gathered disciples, in some cases they even took their money. Then, they feed them a batch of pre-packaged nonsense that they read in some book or heard from some other teacher. I call this, *"Borrowed knowledge."*

This is particularly the case with what may be termed the, *"New Age Guru."* As the majority of them have never spend long years in a monastery or as a *sadhu* truly mastering the essence of whatever school of thought they would later teach, they do not possess a deeper understanding of Absolute Truth. Though, they will of course deny this fact. Instead, these teachers personally decide that they know enough to teach; decide that they have the gift of teaching. From this, they move forwards telling people how they should live their lives.

The reason this is so wrong is that if, for example, you teach someone how to read, all of his or her life becomes better and more fulfilled. But, if someone is telling another person how to encounter interpersonal relationships, how they should behave in a particular life-circumstance, or even how they should live their life on a day-to-day basis, all they are basing this advice upon in their own personal perspective of this place we call, *"Life."* Thus, by its very nature this advice is flawed by the *guru's* own personality.

This is why so many people have become so upset at their one-time *guru.* ...Because all they were given was advice based upon how a specific individual expected another person to behave. The information that they were provided with was not based on a truly enlightened perspective.

As a young adolescent on the *Spiritual Path* I grew up at a time and in a place where there was a lot of opportunity to meet and interact with spiritual teachers. The majority of the teachers I encountered and interacted with were from various realms of Asia. Certainly, most prominently, I was very close with Swami Satchidananda. I can tell you, that not one time did he or any of these other teachers ever tell me how to live my life. They never gave me their opinion about what I should do next. If I asked them a question, they would turn it around on me and inquiring what I truly desired. From this, as I was never told what to do, I was simply allowed to chart my own personal path. This is true spiritual teaching. These are the true spiritual teachers.

A true *guru* does not tell you what to do or how to do it, even if you ask. A true *guru* does not tell you what he or she thinks you should do. A true *guru* allows you to be you.

Stop wasting your time listening to people who are not themselves complete. All you are doing is feeding their ego and maybe even their wallet. At the end of the day, though they may be momentarily telling you what you want to hear, you will be left misguided because you did not come to true-knowledge on your own.

## What Are You Basing Your Knowledge Upon?

It is a curious condition of life, but people base what they think they know upon what they heard from some other person, who heard it from another person, who heard it from who knows where... Most people never base their beliefs upon the source of the information.

People spend their entire existence thinking that they know something. But, how do they know it? They think they know it because they heard it from a secondhand source. Or, they heard it from someone who had an agenda.

This is not knowledge. This is rumor. This is speculation. In some cases, this is a lie.

Even if we go to the foundation of religious and moral culture, we are still not at the source. Jesus did not write *the Bible.* Buddha did not write *the Dhammapada.* People wrote those books. People who claimed to know what Jesus or the Buddha said and believed. But, did those people who wrote the scriptures actually know what Jesus or the Buddha said or thought? Or, did they simply want to project their own ideologies into what became these holy teaching?

Throughout our existence, in this place we call life, we will each come upon our beliefs. We will come upon them from various sources. In most cases, once a person believes something, it will be impossible to make them stop their belief. This is where the problems with truth arise.

Is belief a truth? No, it is simply a belief.

Most people spend their entire life believing what they hear and not questioning the source. From this, untruths and lies are perpetuated throughout this life-scape. This pattern makes no-thing in life better.

Therefore, before you ever decide to believe anything, go to the source. Not only will this make you a person who bases their beliefs upon foundational evidence, but it will also make this life-place much better because it will end the spread of falsehoods based upon hearsay.

Who do you want to be? Do you want to be a person who knows the truth or do you want to be a person who bases their life upon falsehoods?

## *What If You Didn't Know?*

Whenever you are upset about something, (no matter what that something is), there is one common denominator to the equation, *You Know.*

Think about this, *"What if you didn't know?"*

If you didn't know then you would not be upset about whatever it is you are upset about. And, the only reason you are upset is because you know about something that makes you angry, unhappy, sad, depressed, or whatever. Something OUT THERE is causing you to lose your peace.

How many times in your life has something been going on for a day, a week, a month, a year and you didn't know about it? Throughout all that time your life was fine. Then, you found out about it, and you became enraged. Though it was already going on, you didn't know, so you didn't care.

It is an obvious expression of life for us to be unhappy about something that we are unhappy about. But, the main point is, all life is based on you. Just because you don't like something doesn't mean that the person next to you will not like it. Just as because something makes you angry does not mean that the same thing would make anyone else angry.

That being said, there are things that anger us all. But, it is essential to note that your life and your emotions are defined by you. How you decide to feel about any particular issues is also defined by you.

There are obvious things that would make any of us mad if that THING was directed in our direction. But, how we chose to deal with that anger makes us who we are. This choice of dealing is also how we each set the next set of events in motion in our lives and the lives of others involved with us or involved with the issue.

Anger can only equal so much. Understanding this, how you deal with your anger is what defines you as a person.

Do you internalize and simply sit around mad? That is understood to not be psychologically good for a person.

Do you react and take over-exaggerated reactions? Meaning, do you do something destructive when you get mad? That's not good either because that type of reactive action can have devastating effects upon your life.

Do you take concise positive action to undo the negative or destructive actions of others? That's probably the best action to take, if you decided to take action at all. But, that's not easy. Most people who do something that will make you angry do not care how you feel, or they would not have done it in the first place. If they cared, they would care about you.

If someone doesn't care about the effect of what they are doing may be having on another person, or on the greater scheme of things, that means they only care about themselves. And sadly, this is one of the biggest faults of the human condition; selfishness and not caring.

So here, we get back to the main point – what if you didn't know?

Is there a way to erase your knowing? I think if this were possible most of us would erase a lot of the things that have happened to us or the horrible things that we have seen, heard about, or have lived. But, I do not think that it is doable—at least not in this day or age. So, we are stuck. We can pretend that we don't know, but that is only pretending—we still know.

Ultimately, all we can do is to do what we can do as consciously as possible and then let it go. Though letting go is, *"Not knowing."* But, if we can let it go long enough maybe the bad things or the bad people that have made us angry will fade away; captured by their own negative actions.

## *Just Because You Pass the Information Onto Somebody Doesn't Mean That They Understand It*

You can teach people things. You can tell them how to do things. You can make them repeat what they have learned but that does not mean that they understand what you have taught them.

Understanding is very different from memorizing facts. Understanding is based upon personal realization.

We each have our teachers. They may guide us on the road to understanding by teaching us what they have learned. But, it is only when we come to our own realizations about the words and the techniques that have been presented to us, that we truly realize knowledge.

It is for this reason that in many spiritual traditions they say, *"There are no secrets."* Why? Because there aren't. The information is out there. It is already presented. But, simply because it is presented and some people may even be able recite it verbatim, this does not mean that they truly understand what they are repeating—it does not mean that they truly comprehend the subtleties.

Realization is based upon processing the information presented to you and making it whole and complete within yourself.

Become realized.

## *You Get What You Pay For*

Bad things happen to good people. When this occurs, there is nothing right about it on any level.

Bad things also happen to not so good people. When this occurs, the recipients of these situations usually reach out, and they receive sympathy from family and friends.

Bad things happen to bad people. But, that somehow seems right and just. No one offers them sympathy.

It is never fun to receive anything bad in life. But, people set their own life-course in motion. If a person is negative, critical, judgmental, violent, or cruel, and then draws attention to themselves and what they are doing, it is just the reality of life—their actions will cause reactions and negative people and events will accost them.

There are a lot of crazy people in the world. They do bad, mean-spirited things; motivated by a selfish, power-hungry mindset. It is not right but it is the way it is.

If you draw negative attention to yourself, this is the type of person who will seek you out. If you are hurting people, animals, or this life-place, and not caring about your actions, what reaction do you think you will encounter?

It is for this reason, if you wish to limit the amount of unnecessary bad-things you will be accosted by in life, you must set your life-course for only doing good things: being good, saying good things, helping people, and leaving any place you visit better from your presence. Forget about desired fame, fortune, position, title, and/or psychological justifications for doing what you're doing—because at the end of the day that is all nonsense. If you want a good life, it is simple, DO GOOD THINGS!

I've said it a lot of times before, it is very obvious what is good and what is bad. If what you are doing hurts someone or something, it is bad. If what you are doing hurts no one and no-thing and helps this Life-Place, it is good.

If you do good things, good things will follow you. You get what you pay for.

## *How You Measure Time?*

Each of us has a moment that we call our Life-Time. In that timeframe we do what we do and then WE are gone. Much of life is spent taking care of the necessities: putting a roof over our heads, feeding our loved ones and ourselves, and taking care of business. Some of us are lucky, we like what we are doing while we are taking care of the necessities. For others, this is not the case. But, at the end of the day, how we spend our Life-Time is how we spent our Life-Time. Love it, hate it, when it is over it is over and that is that. Though we may be remembered, WE are gone. So, all that takes place after our physical existence doesn't really matter – at least not to US.

I have discussed TIME is several places, most notability my book, *Zen O'clock: Time to Be*. Time and how we live it is a very interesting subject. Take, for example a café that you go into all the time. The staff knows you. Then, you are gone for a month or more. When you return and the staff greets you, they do so as if you were never away. Why is this? Because they are locked into the time and space of the reality of the café; all they do is based upon that denominator. They know you from there. They see you there. Time passes and they take no notice of the time passing or your away-ness. When you return, they are simply seeing you THERE again. Thus, you were never gone.

We each want to live our Life-Time in a certain manner. We each want to make our Life-Time count. We want to live it well—be fulfilled, be happy, and exist in our own suchness. Most people are not afforded this luxury, however. They are dominated by culture, they give into the daily grind, and they go through their days in a daze; believing in the promise of the Some-Time and the Some-Day. Thus, they are lost to True Reality and their TIME simply goes by. Others get what they want—at least so they think. But, what they WANT ultimately robs their time and at the end of their days their time was gone just as everyone else's but because they believed their needs were being answered it took them too long to realize the lie of their own Life-Time—*that getting what you think you want answers the true desire of forever fulfilled time.*

So, what is left? How can you live your Life-Time? How can you live your short moment of life to the fullest? How can you be HERE in the NOW?

The ultimate answer is you can't. Your human form defines you. You are defined by the length of your Life-Time and the opportunities and availabilities presented to you in that space of reality. You are defined by where you find yourself in time, space, culture, and socioeconomic availabilities. Thus, you are never wholly you. You are, at best, what you convince yourself to be or, more than likely, what you pretend to be.

Happy or sad... Those are temporal emotions. Fulfillment is simply having your momentary desires met. Fulfillment is not True Understanding.

Life is an illusion defined by time. When your time is up, your illusion will end.

## Hello! This is Reality

All forms of spirituality are an attempt for humanity to find an explanation for the *What is* and *Why*. All forms of religion attempt to harness the concept of a Supreme Being and bottle it up so that people will fall into line and believe what the specific religion believes that they should believe.

When we look back in history, we see that many cultures worshiped various forms of the gods in everything from the weather, to nature, and all kinds of variations of what we now call, *"Pagan idols."* When the modern person views these peoples they think, *"How naïve."*

As modern spirituality took hold in the late nineteenth century, all kinds of philosophies were disseminated. Some called this period, *The Age of Aquarius*. It later became more commonly know as, *The New Age*. And, in time, I am certain a new name will be applied. But, what is now taught is not dissimilar to the ancient religious traditions of worshiping the wind or various physical elements that were said to embody certain mystical powers and then taking specific magical actions in order to invoke various cosmic energies to bring about the desired results into your life.

Throughout this modern *New Age* timeframe, all kinds of metaphysical *mumbo-jumbo* has been taught. People are told to wear amulets, hang crystals, do little mini-magic ceremonies, place coins at the feet of divine statues, and recite positive affirmations with the hope that what a person wants will be brought into their life. At the heart of all of this is the fact that most people are dissatisfied with their lives and they want something more. And, motivating all of this are the teachers of this mumbo-jumbo. They are the ones writing the books, giving the lectures, and making the promises that this or that will work in obtaining desired end-goals. They do this while they are also the ones making the money and getting their egos stroked by all the dissatisfied people out there seeking a new promise.

What's wrong with this equitation?

The fact of the matter is, everybody wants something more or something different in their life. But, amulets, chants, magical ceremonies, or wall hangings of Jesus, Krishna, or the Buddha are not going to bring it to you. What will bring it to you is cleaning yourself up, getting yourself straight. Meaning, getting rid of all the things that hold you back from being who you want to be and getting what you want out of life.

Stop pretending that you are something you are not. Stop lying to yourself that some amulet, some affirmation, some *mantra,* or some magic ceremony will bring what you want into your life. Get psychological help if you need it to fix the flaws in your personality. Go to school and learn what you need to learn to take the next step in your life. Do what you need to do to make yourself physically, mentally, and psychologically ENOUGH to step towards your dreams. But, ultimately remember the profound words of the Buddha, *"The cause of suffering is desire."* Stop desiring and everything else, all the nonsense of the world, falls away.

## *You'll See When You See.*
## *You'll Know When You Know.*

When we are young most of us are open to new thought, philosophies, and ideas. When we are young it is simply more of a condition of lack of life experience, before the *samsara* has been cut too deeply into our brains, which causes us to listen and try to understand what others think and believe. Give it a few years though, and most of us have already made up our minds. With this, it becomes very hard to get someone to listen and understand new ideologies.

From our earliest years forward, we are programmed by our parents, our family, our friends, and our culture to believe certain things. In some rare cases children are actually taught to explore new thoughts and ideologies at every opportunity. But, this is rarely the case. Most youthful programing is much more dogmatic than that. From this dogmatic programing, we seal off our minds to new thoughts and ideas.

Right or wrong, positive or negative, truth or lies does not matter. We already know all we need to know. Any new idea that we hear is simply dismissed.

This is a sad and debilitating Life-Condition. As so much is lost. So, many new and expansive avenues are never explored because the pathway is dismissed before it is ever experienced.

This is also why so many people never find their own voice or their own creativity because they set about on a path of dismissal before any new idea can be comprehended, let alone be explored or understood.

It is from this mindset that people spend their life defined solely by what they think about others: what others have done, what others have accomplished, what others have created. Thus, true personal Life-Experience and Creativity is never found.

Do you spend your life creating? Or, do you spend your life discussing what others have created?

Do you already know, or do you experience?

## The Earth Still Spins

Whenever something traumatic or all-encompassing happens to you or something you care about, all of your attention is focused upon THAT. You are sad, you are upset, you are angry; you may even want to get revenge. What has happened has caused you to become very One-Pointed. But, no matter how much something that has happened to you or someone or something you care about may emotionally affect and control you, the earth still spins—the rest of the world goes on and no one else knows or even cares about how you feel.

This is one of the main things that you have to realize in life if you hope to pass through it with any level of refined consciousness. You have to understand that no matter how big the tragedy; other things are happening all across the globe that probably dwarf whatever happened to you.

Even in the case when some large catastrophe has occurred, most of the world still does not have a T.V or the Internet so even if they do hear about it, they cannot take the time to care, because they are surround by famine, by poverty, by violence, by war, or simply they need to go to work every day to make ends meet. Thus, they cannot take the time to care.

People really get locked into their own head when they do not like what has happened to them or to someone whom they may care about. But, people can only behave in that manner when they have the time, the money, and the emotional support to do so. They can only care when they do not have to worry about their own survival. They can only care when they have nothing better to do.

Think about this, if you have to focus on your everyday survival would you care about the small things that you care about? Could you care about those things if you have no place to live, no food to eat, and no one to care that you care?

It really is a simple equation. And, you need to think about this before you spend the time and the emotional energy to be dominated by anything that is not Life-Essential.

Life is life. We pass through it. Things happen that we do not like to all of us.

Are you and your actions defined by those things? Or, are you more than that? Do they control you or do you control them?

Life and consciously living life on this planet is more than simply defined by how you feel about some event in the life of one person.

Seek something bigger than being focused upon you. That is *The Greater Pathway*.

# THE ZEN

## Books By Scott Shaw Include:

About Peace:
A 108 Ways to Be At Peace
When Things Are Out of Control
Advanced Taekwondo
Arc Left from Istanbul
Bangkok and the Nights of Drunken Stupor
Bangkok: Beyond the Buddha
Bus Rides
Cambodian Refugees in Long Beach, California: The Definitive Study
Chi Kung For Beginners
China Deep
e.q.
Essence: The Zen of Everything
Hapkido: Articles on Self-Defense
Hapkido: Essays on Self-Defense
Hapkido: The Korean Art of Self Defense
Hong Kong: Out of Focus
Independent Filmmaking: Secrets of the Craft
Israel in the Oblique
Junk: The Backstreets of Bangkok
Last Will and Testament According to the Divine Rite of the Drug Cocaine
L.A.: Tales from the Suburban Side of Hell
Marguerite Duras and Charles Bukowski:
    The Yin and Yang of Modern Erotic Literature
Mastering Health: The A to Z of Chi Kung
Nirvana in a Nutshell
No Kisses for the Sinner
On the Hard Edge of Hollywood

*Pagan Burma: Shadows of the Stupa*
*Sake' in a Glass, Sushi with Your Fingers:*
*Fifteen Minutes in Tokyo*
*Samurai Zen*
*Scream of the Buddha*
*Scribbles on the Restroom Wall*
*Sedona: Realm of the Vortex*
*Shama Baba*
*Shanghai Whispers Shanghai Screams*
*Shattered Thoughts*
*Singapore Off Center*
*South Korea: In a Blur*
*Suicide Slowly*
*Taekwondo Basics*
*Taekwondo: Fifty Essential Techniques*
*The Ki Process:*
*Korean Secrets for Cultivating Dynamic Energy*
*The Little Book of Yoga Breathing*
*The Little Book of Yoga Meditation*
*The Little Book of Zen Mediation*
*The Lyrics*
*The Most Beautiful Woman in Shanghai*
*The Passionate Kiss of Illusion*
*The Screenplays*
*The Tao of Chi*
*The Tao of Self-Defense*
*The Warrior is Silent:*
   *Martial Arts and the Spiritual Path*
*TKO: A Lost Night in Tokyo*
*Wet Dreams and Placid Silence*
*Yoga: The Inner Journey*
*Yoga: The Spiritual Aspects*

*Zen and Modern Consciousness*
*Zen Buddhism: The Pathway to Nirvana*
*Zen Filmmaking*
*Zen in the Blink of an Eye*
*Zen O'clock: Time to Be*
*Zen: Tales from the Journey*
*Zero One*

www.ingramcontent.com/pod-product-compliance
Lightning Source LLC
Chambersburg PA
CBHW061759110426
42742CB00012BB/2183